TIMESTRAPPING

How startups can create more time to take on and
take down the competition

Brent Daily

Edited by Ellen Neuborne
Designed by Katie Genauer

Brent Daily
TimeStrapping
©2020, Epicentered
Boulder, CO
timestrappingbook.com
All rights reserved.

First tip: Don't waste time reading this page.

DEAR FOUNDER

I hadn't planned on spending my birthday morning sitting in a dark alcove just off the lobby of Boulder's nicest hotel. Yet, there I was. Getting fired from the company I started. The news, delivered without an ounce of coffee or empathy, tore me apart.

I'd sacrificed years of salary, thought about little else for more than six years, and done things miles out of my comfort zone for the company. I was hurt. I felt like a failure.

The company pre-dated my children, so it felt like I'd lost one of them. I wasn't just angry; I was blindingly furious. The nicest thing I could think of saying before walking away was, "don't f--- this up."

More than anything, I felt cheated. I had drunk the Kool-Aid.

From accelerators to business schools to oceans of digital ink, I'd followed the narrative told to startup founders. We'd listened to prospects, slaved over the product, reduced the friction to use it as much as possible, experimented with various sales approaches, started hammering on the use case where we fit the market, and the list went on.

But none of it mattered.

I felt cheated because I came to realize that the general narrative in the startup community was, not wrong, but woefully incomplete.

The clinical approach of being lean, performing customer discovery, finding product-market fit, etc. all matter. There are books and blogs aplenty about how you should run your business. But the path to addressing those challenges lies more within the founder than it does in the process.

Those frameworks to build a company demand a founder ask smart questions, listen, and quickly find new solutions. But those are table stakes.

Anyone can do those. And everyone should.

A startup isn't like building Ikea furniture. You don't just ask question A during customer discovery, hear answer B, and build product C in order to create product-market fit. If it were that easy *successful* startups would be as prevalent as the Poäng armchair.

Two things are missing from all that advice.

One is the value of time. The other, the importance of the mental game.

The successful entrepreneurs who penned those frameworks fail to acknowledge how unique they are. It's their own mentality that was their brilliance and allowed the frameworks to succeed, not the framework itself. They're successful because of how they valued time and how that guided their decision-making.

What makes time and a founder's mentality even more critical is that failing the mental game costs you time. It's like cutting the wrong wire when diffusing the bomb and the red numbers on the digital timer just start ticking down at 2x speed.

A CEO's job, as the old axe goes, is to *make sure you never run out of money.*

That's an unbreakable golden rule. There aren't even exceptions to prove it. But a startup never feels like it has money so, while true, it's not the resource that's common to every decision.

That resource is time.

Sitting in that hallway, between the multi-million-dollar views of the mountains and the soulless conference rooms that could have been in any chain hotel in the world, the clock struck triple zeroes. My time was up, pencils down.

I'd failed to recognize that we were in the time business. Every startup is. You're starting from way behind and dealing with bigger, better resourced competitors. While we often deride the speed of Corporate America in startup land, they've learned to run (or at least walk briskly).

As startups, we may run faster, but we've spotted our corporate competitors an unfathomable head start. They're clear over the horizon, having learned what the market needs and what to say in order to get people to buy their product.

The tortoise wins in the fable because he doesn't waste time, not just because he was persistent.

Time, not money, allows us to catch them. The longer the race, the better our odds.

The founder's job is actually to *extend the race as long as possible.*

Building a product takes longer than anyone estimates. Scheduling the meeting with a prospect takes weeks longer than it should. Learning how to actually hear your prospects takes dozens, if not hundreds, of meetings. Finding people who want to help you *and are good* is a full-time job in itself.

But, most importantly, trying something new that could be the exponential game-changing idea demands time. So too does recovering should it fail.

Everything. Takes. Time.

I can hear your thoughts. That's what money is for, right? Money buys you people which buys more time to experiment.

And it is true, money certainly helps. But it's a function of time and can only do so much. Money can't help you make better decisions, prevent you from exploring dead end ideas, or help you waste less time. Money can't truncate the disagreement on direction with your founders or coax the next great idea out of an employee.

Beyond having enough to meet the bottom of Maslow's hierarchy, money is an amplifier. If you know how to make money it can help you make more. If you don't yet, it can exacerbate bad decisions by wasting everyone's time.

That's where the mental game is vital.

It's not the frameworks that matter as much as the mentality with which we approach the new information, how we determine what matters, and how we decide to focus our time and energy.

Every startup is different.

Luck matters. Timing matters. Macro-economic conditions matter. Competitive landscapes matter.

But what matters most is *you*.

It's your approach to the blank slate, it's how you respond to hearing 'no' thousands of times or having users tell you that your product sucks (some in choicer words than that), and it's your ability to grind through the hard stuff instead of chasing the next shiny object that matters.

It's all about you and no framework will increase your odds of success until you understand yourself and those around you.

Everyone has their holes. Some of which we're aware, others not. The ones we recognize tend to be a lack of knowledge and are easily solved. Mentors and content can fill those gaps because we know the hole that needs filling and are receptive to filling it.

The others are truly blind spots. Not only do we not know they exist, but we're reticent to acknowledge them because we can easily rationalize our existing viewpoints. These are mental holes and are the ones that kill our companies.

In my case, I needed something from my startup experience that went deeper than an exit. I needed someone to validate me. Just tell me that I'm smart and that you're amazed at how much of the water I could carry. Please.

Even a decade later, that's a difficult and ugly truth to admit. Back then it'd have been impossible to admit. It's also why the sting of getting fired was the most painful experience of my life. It was the exact opposite of the thing I couldn't admit I needed. I had lost.

I couldn't properly apply any of the frameworks because I'd seen the future, a future where our company had made a monster impact, and it was real.

I'd assumed the time to get from here to there was a given. That assumption led me to pursue paths that mattered and created value, but those paths actually mattered less and created less value than the ones that would have bought time. My ego, my insecurities, made it more difficult to sell because I needed the approach (and thus me) validated rather simply the sale. I didn't learn to shut up and would talk right through the yes.

The mental game is more than ego, however. The mental game allows for an objectivity that helps you evaluate which of the paths available to you will buy your company more time. It's knowing why your default is to build the next feature instead of trying to get 100 people to buy the product as it is and then removing what you want from the equation to determine what the company needs.

The startup path has thousands of forks in its journey.

Each fork is a decision point. Some of the paths are dead ends, some meander for months before you realize they're a dead end, and others can buy you a few extra hours of life.

The mental game is not easy to describe and is intertwined with every facet of your business from what you decide to work on to how you engage your employees to how you find value in your board meetings.

Again. Your job is to extend the race. Buy time so you can generate more value.

What matters is having a mentality that recognizes how precious that time is and optimizing it for everyone in your orbit. That's what's missing from most startup advice.

It's fun to read about the startups who seemingly did everything right so long as you recognize it for the fictional escapism it is. A couple companies every year will have the exact right product at the exact right time and become order takers. They print time because everyone's throwing money at them in order to use the product. They're called unicorns for a reason.

For the other 99.9999% of us there's hard work, punishing self-doubt, constant distractions, and hitting the refresh button with hopes the customer's check will clear before payroll is deducted.

The purpose of this book is to help you avoid some of the common, unforced, mental errors that we create for ourselves, as well as the errors we make because we're doing something for the first (or second) time. *Timestrapping* is meant to help you think through your strategic dilemmas in ways that allow you to find a solution that works for the specific conditions you face.

This is by no means a magic bullet. Quite the opposite.

Timestrapping is about evaluating the paths you may reflexively choose in order to see the ones that create time.

What follows is an accumulation of advice that I've been given, advice I've given out, or things I learned over years of self-flagellation while stewing over all the things I wish I'd done differently. Some of the advice is obvious, some contrarian. But all of it has been battle tested.

Your time is invaluable, and that time is wasted if you're given advice when you're not ready.

With that, please do *not* feel the need to read this from front to back. Reading cover to cover is a terribly inefficient use of your time.

Just read the table of contents.

If you're wrestling with something in particular or something strikes a chord, flip to that page to get another perspective about how to think about it and some ideas on how to execute.

I hope the five-minutes required to read a section can buy you back weeks in return. And I hope that time leads you to success and not the dark alcove of a hotel hallway.

Good luck,
+brent

TABLE OF CONTENTS

YOU

Starting a company can be depressingly difficult. Quite literally. Entrepreneurs are three-times more likely to suffer from depression than others.

I am one.

I hit my low the week after my first child was born. The same week my first company entered one of the first Techstars accelerator cohorts. That was the week I finally admitted I needed some help.

I was in uncharted territory without the swagger to move forward. I didn't know what to do or where to focus my energy.

I dreaded being asked what was happening with the company. I couldn't help but think: Is it really a company when you're not making any progress?

Fortunately, I met a co-founder. Though we came to a disastrous ending, the company would never have gotten going without his brute-force energy. It took getting that giant flywheel inching along for me to get going myself. Once I saw movement, the next step became a little clearer. I came out from hiding behind researching the product to helping build and sell it.

But that depression never went away because I always felt like we were being chased. We needed to move faster to box out competition or be smarter to get more adoption. It was a treadmill that never stopped.

If I could go back in time and relive those days, I absolutely would. But I wish I could do it again with the knowledge I have today. Not just the operational knowledge to focus our efforts or the experience to see the market for what it truly was, but the psychological knowledge to have better managed myself.

Thankfully, not everyone goes through that.

The biggest challenge (for me) was ginning up that effort every day. It meant waging battle with the soundtrack in my head: punishing self-doubt, withering self-criticism, and even subconscious self-sabotage.

The collection of pieces that follow are the criticisms that played on my soundtrack and the advice I'd give to the 30-something me about how to manage my energy, how to give myself credit for what's going well, and how to reframe the stories I was telling myself so I could give everything I had every day.

Our internal criticisms waste valuable time by unnecessarily punishing and demotivating. Even though we gut it out and power ahead, the soundtrack plays on. Addressing it now and giving ourselves permission to change how we view progress and view ourselves can help to overcome the mental strawman of being an imposter-preneur.

Yes, having a high bar is required. Holding ourselves accountable is required. Constant learning and improvement are required. But don't mistake mental self-bullying as a fulfillment of those requirements.

We wouldn't manage an employee via constant negative performance reviews, yet many of us believe that's how we bring out the best in ourselves.

Instead, it deflates us, gets us spending the time we have less productively, and clouds our ability to prioritize because we're too busy beating ourselves up about that thing we did (or didn't do) yesterday.

Time is a resource, but it's only valuable if we have the tools to use it well.

QUESTIONING YOURSELF

Your self-doubt holds you back from putting your idea and yourself out into the world. You probably don't believe that, but I'm willing to bet that you said you have to improve just one thing *before* you promote your product, talk to that investor, or try to sell to that interested customer.

You have to feel like what you're doing is real before others will have the confidence to buy.

The bar that makes your company real is different for everyone. It may be centered around a product milestone, having closed funding, reaching a revenue threshold, or simply having business cards.

As an early first-time entrepreneur, my days were riddled with self-doubt, mental lashings, and hopelessness. I didn't know what needed my focus and, on the off chance I did, I didn't exactly know what I was doing.

I spent three days working on a name and another day working on a logo. Over half a week on something that didn't build a product or convince anyone that someday they should pay me a dollar. I had fun doing it all, but it left me in despair. Further evidence that I was a hack, the voice in my head never failed to tauntingly remind.

Ultimately, the name proved useful. Everyone loved it and immediately understood why we did what we did.

It wasn't a waste of time at all. Perhaps a true product person or investor would say it was done out of order but, most importantly, it started to make things real for me.

When people asked what I was working on, I could tell them I'd started a company called RoundPegg. They could go to a website and check it out. It became tangible and, if it didn't build my confidence, it at least made me feel a bit less like an imposter-preneur.

That's invaluable.

Your brain is your own worst enemy. The sneaky part is that it knows where all your weaknesses are and, if you're prone to listening to the voice it pokes those weaknesses with a sharp stick every hour. That voice will drive you crazy. For every counterargument you know to be true, your brain is a step ahead and can parry all attempts to stay positive.

It doesn't matter whether you've been at this for a day or a decade. Your mind will be your best foil or your greatest advocate of unwarranted hubris.

Your competition is almost always yourself.

If you can find ways to congratulate yourself on the smallest bits of progress and come back to do it all again the next day, you're winning. What separates you from people smarter and more talented is your willingness to come back and do it again.

Consider These Actions:

- Dig deep to understand what will make you feel like you have created a real company. Then do it.
    - Publish your website.
    - Order a business card.
    - Speak at a local event, to a local company, or host a webinar.
    - Use different words – "I started a company…," not "I'm starting…" Be definitive. Your words matter, especially to the voice in your head.
- Invest in design so you look like your company belongs. This is where the 'fake it 'til you make it' mentality is actually constructive. When your presence in the world makes you look like a company of hundreds, then you're credible. The inner critic gets easier to defeat when the words and actions of others are aligned to prove it false.

FACING ENDLESS TASKS

There is never a lack of things to do. The more you beat yourself up about the lack of accomplishments, the less motivated you are to tick the next box. The feeling of helplessness is a negative loop. You are in control of your effort, focus, and motivation.

Creating a positive cycle is easier said than done. But it must be done.

At the 'end' of a workday, it's easy to focus on the myriad tasks that still have to be accomplished. The list is so long that knocking a few things off doesn't move the needle enough to feel good about your efforts.

This is infinitely more true in the early days when *everything* has to get done.

Your options are either to push many rocks up the hill a few feet each or to push one rock all the way up.

Only you know how you react to each and which gives you a greater sense of accomplishment. But, mentally, something 90% complete is the same as something 0% done. The weight of incompleteness isn't any lighter.

Try limiting your scope. Pick the top three and define what is 'good enough.' Because you'll never give yourself credit for great, don't hold that as the bar.

Get to 'good enough' and move on. Odds are that you'll look at them in a year and want to redo them anyway.

Sisyphean efforts feel better when you can *feel* the progress. If you're going to push 100 rocks up a hill, I'd encourage you to push them one at a time.

Focusing is critical. You only have so much mental bandwidth. If your mind is constantly 'multi-tasking' and juggling tasks, you're operating well below your optimal level. Put pen to paper and give yourself permission to tackle it later.

Consider These Actions:
- Push one rock all the way up the hill. Finish the feat so you can let go.
- Write down *one* thing you will accomplish today. (If it's big, write down the milestone you'll meet on the path to complete.). Just one. Get it done. You won't call it a day if you complete it before lunch so there's no

downside. The upside is that you won't mentally tar and feather yourself if it takes all day to complete.

- Pre-define 'good enough' for each task and allow it to be so.
- When you think of a task, write it down so it doesn't take up space on your mental hard drive.

CONTROLLING YOUR DAY

There are so many tasks you could undertake on any given day that it can be paralyzing. If you can't dictate your day, the feeling of having made no progress will only reinforce any negative thoughts in your head.

You can only accomplish so much. That's true whether you plan or not. But the purpose of planning is psychological, not just executional. When you're in control you at least give yourself a shot at having an accomplishment that can carry you through to begin the next day.

We've all felt the dread of work. Those times when we open the computer and aren't quite sure what to do next. The quantity of tasks can be overwhelming when every one of them is on the table.

Getting started is more than picking one. Without finding a way to let the others lay quietly at your feet they'll be leaping up, begging for attention and constantly reminding you that they're equally important.

For me, taking control of my day required three things:

1. Identifying the (singular) most important thing on which to work that day;
2. Giving myself permission to let the others lie; and
3. Calming my brain to reduce the constant anxiety of not doing enough and to allow myself time to relax and focus.

The best approach, in my case, was to create a pre-game ritual to prepare myself mentally and tactically for the day.

If you've played sports you likely had a pre-game ritual that got you ready to go— not just physically, but mentally. I did, and while I didn't always play well, I was at least prepared.

My routine is short(ish) so I can do it every day. It includes a few minutes of:

* meditating to quell my anxiety;
* listening to what the 80-year-old me would tell myself to give me the wisdom of hindsight and connect with what I value;

- revisiting the big picture (what work is important to meet the next milestone); and

- scheduling the day in half-hour increments.

Your routine will vary but do something that makes you feel like you're in control—not just of the day, but of your emotions.

The simple act of taking the reins is a major stress reliever.

Consider These Actions:

- Find a daily ritual that *relaxes* you to start your day.

- Take out your to-do list and identify the most important item. Then start a new list for the day that cuts what you think is realistic in half. These are the ones to which you'll hold yourself accountable to today. (There are always little things that just have to happen, like returning a phone call. Some people find the 1-3-5 strategy to be helpful: Do one big task, three mediums, and five small ones.)

- Plan your day to the half-hour. The purpose isn't to live like a robot but to give yourself the permission to take time for yourself and to create reasonable expectations. It's the unmet expectations that are the gas can for your stress.

- Write your job description. When you're responsible for everything, you don't really have a job; you have *every* job. Give yourself a job in order to focus your mind as you walk through your door.

FEELING GUILTY THINKING

As an early-stage CEO, the second most important job you have, next to not running out of money, is to do everything you can to help the team execute. That could be you and your co-founder or a team of dozens.

Execution starts with focus.

One of the most effective things you can do is to take some time to synthesize everything you've learned: what competitors are doing, what you've heard from prospects, where your team is getting tripped up, etc.

Processing information helps to avoid reacting. When you're reacting, you're willingly playing by the rules of the incumbents. Reacting is only worthwhile when you're in the lead. When you're still catching up, you need to impart your will on the competition to get them to play from your playbook rather than the one they've spent months or years designing for themselves.

The hardest part of taking the time to think is giving yourself the permission to do so. Just because you aren't in the office and just because your computer is closed doesn't mean you aren't creating value.

The value of thinking is the ability to:

Simplify. Rarely do we spend time reducing our vision. Ideas are additive. Having too many possibilities usually results in the team pulling in different directions. Shrink your vision to fit the near-term.

Say No. Prioritize. There are hundreds of good ideas you could pursue. Only thinking through a framework against which you can say 'no' will help you execute by not pursuing every one of them.

When all good ideas *can* get pursued, there is no avenue not worth exploring. While companies can find 'accidental' success, you're not Columbus. Mistakenly bumping into a different landmass may have been success for him. But luck is a terrible strategy.

The need to stop and think was never more apparent in my career than while working with a high-flying startup that had just closed a $25 million round. "Revenue is a four-letter word. We'll worry about that in [five years]."

This was the CEO's mantra. The idea that we just needed to focus on building something unique and cool ruled the day.

While the money was in the bank, that was fine. But nobody quite knew what their job actually was.

A few months into my tenure, a teammate and I were given the green light to take a week to vet the market and identify a common focus.

Literally three-hours into the week, the plug was pulled. The reason was because there was too much to do to sit around thinking. This was laziness, not action. "This is your problem. You're a thinker and not a doer," the CEO told me.

The story didn't end well for that company. After raising tens of millions, it was acqui-hired at the cost of retention bonuses for the engineers. Having good people around is meaningless if they aren't driving toward a common goal.

There is value in winnowing and giving yourself the quiet time to take a step back. It helps you, but it also helps you scale because you're not scrambling to manually course correct people every single day.

Consider These Actions:

- Keep a running list of possibilities (i.e. potential areas of focus) so you don't feel like you're ignoring something critical.
- Put two hours on your calendar every week to step back and reevaluate the priorities. Nothing will burn down in two hours.
- Find a mentor with whom you can take an hour every couple of weeks to help solidify the priorities. An objective perspective can see things you can't. You're too close.

MAINTAINING OPTIMISM

There will always be things that must improve. As you learn more and connect new dots, you'll generate new ideas.

Execution will never keep pace with observation.

If you let the myriad things that are wrong scream louder than the few things that are right, motivation will be harder to come by for both you and the team.

You will always focus on the squeaky wheels. That's what will make you better. But taking the time to acknowledge that you've created the wheel in the first place will power you through to fix the squeak.

You have two options.

One, focus on the delta between your current state and perfection and fall short every single day. You'll drive hard and never be happy. That gap between the vision and reality is a cortisol faucet in your brain. It stunts creativity and creates yet another hurdle to overcome. And if you have employees, it's not a terribly fun environment in which to operate when you're recognized not for what you've accomplished but for what you need to fix next.

Or two, keep perfect in mind and mentally reward yourself (and others) for making progress toward it every day. You wouldn't have started something if you didn't hold yourself to a high bar. Finding drive shouldn't ever be a problem. But lasting motivation and effort always is. Focusing on the improvements you made between yesterday and today is a constructive measurement that drips the dopamine that fuels tomorrow.

The weight of managing the 1,000 things that are not yet right is heavy. It can close doors to seeing other opportunities because the vision of perfect becomes fixed.

The weight of one is relatively light. One thing can get fixed. Focus there.

When confronted with yet another shortcoming, write it down. Your natural reaction will be to react and make things happen. Resist.

Give yourself permission to solve it later so you can complete the job you've already identified as the most important. Often, what appears urgent today can seem relatively unimportant next week. The world changes frequently when you're a new business.

What you think the solution is today is likely not *the* solution. Things will look different tomorrow after you've learned more about the industry, heard more from prospects, or released a completely unrelated feature. When inputs change, outputs usually change too.

Make progress, yes. But do so thoughtfully in order to keep your sanity and so as not to lose sight of what's vitally important.

Doing so limits your whiplash.

Consider These Actions:
- Keep a list of the broken, forgotten, and ill-conceived. Just don't keep it in your head.
- Keep a list of the positive. Recent wins, good developments, and new ideas are all important to your state of mind.
- Highlight the things that are going or have gone right at your weekly team meeting and only drum on the top one or two things that need improvement. It will help everyone focus and set them up to succeed. One focus, one fix. Many foci, no fixes.

NOTHING SEEMS GOOD ENOUGH

The biggest cost you have as an early stage company isn't your employees' salary, it's their time.

Opportunity costs are enormous, but invisible.

Getting something off the ground requires more than one thing done well. You have to have a story, investor pitch decks, sales collateral, marketing messaging, the product, pricing, case studies, etc. There is no shortage of things that will make that first or next sale smoother.

Your constraint is time. Every time you spend the extra day to polish one thing you lose a day to work on the next.

Generating the first million dollars in revenue requires you to have every piece of the puzzle done well enough, but not done perfectly. There isn't one particular piece, that if expertly nailed, will carry all the others.

You have to be okay putting yourself (and by extension, your product) out there in a way that you know isn't perfect. Truthfully, you don't even know what perfect is yet. The image you have in your mind will be wrong once prospects start asking questions, competitors respond, and you see how someone uses what you've built.

Ultimately, the market will tell you and you'll learn more about what you're doing with every conversation. You'll start to home in on phrases and stories that pique interest or features that could be the springboards to adoption. But you have nothing more than your instinct and educated guesses in the beginning. Those are by no means perfect.

At some point you have to be able to stop building the next thing in order to fix the pieces that got you here. That's another level on your personal permission matrix that needs to be addressed. Later. Much later.

Consider These Actions:
- Listen. Putting something out there at 80% is uncomfortable because it's not representative of the quality you demand, and you fear you'll never get back to it. But the more you put something out and the more you listen; the quicker things get great.

- Find your counterbalance. You aren't the best judge of good enough. Find someone on the team who can carry that flag. Give them the leeway to push things live and make you uncomfortable.
- Reframe the purpose. The goal of getting something into the wild should be to get new information, not to ship it and forget it. Thinking in terms of continual improvement instead of good/bad means you can come back to something.

BUILDING MOMENTUM BY WINNING SMALL

You need to take care of yourself. That means sustaining your confidence and motivation. Nobody will congratulate you on good work, so you must find ways to do that yourself. That means momentarily putting aside all the things you still must accomplish.

In the early days, it's a momentum game. *You* create an outsized amount of that momentum given your energy, drive, and mentality.

But as the months turn to years, you need to find methods to refill your tanks to keep that momentum going.

Winning small can help you find the wins when the larger goals are so daunting. Every week there are steps made toward the larger goal. If you only focus on the big goal, your mentality is that the scoreboard is a switch. You've either made it or you haven't. If you focus on the smaller steps toward that goal, it's a dial. You can see you've made headway and are in a much better position than you were the week before.

Your investors will only focus on the big goals because they're looking ahead toward the next milestone where they can mark up a jump in valuation for their LPs. Using their rubric is a trap. Your goal is to keep the ship on course and the sails full.

When first starting RoundPegg, I read. I searched peer-reviewed psychology databases, printed studies, and read some more. It was several months of not knowing what I was looking for but knowing I'd know it when I found it.

Every day, I felt like a failure. My wife would come home and ask how the day was and I couldn't muster anything positive. Another day without an income, another day spent reading without knowing if I was any closer to finding what I needed.

My greatest accomplishment in those early days was that I'd accumulated a stack of research studies four feet high. I felt like I was wasting time and money, afraid to do something because I didn't know what else to do.

I struggled to stay motivated. I was riding my bike more and 'working' less. Something had to change.

I was focused on the big goal of having a product generating revenue instead of crediting myself for learning and talking to hundreds of experts. Because I was obsessed with the mountain top, I didn't give myself credit for reaching the various camps along the way. The reality is every small step is needed reach the mountain top. My failure to acknowledge the progress nearly shuttered the company before it even started.

The job requires you just keep going. Find ways to recharge and give yourself credit every chance you get.

Consider These Actions:

- Plan your week. Every Sunday evening, identify the smaller steps you want to accomplish (or have the team accomplish) that week. Cut them in half. Revisit on Friday to gauge progress. Track the weeks you nail the goals.

- Get physical. Post goals and timelines on the wall. Make them huge and tactile so you want to play with it, move sticky notes around, or cross things off.

- Cut your monthly goals in half. Eliminating half your goals doesn't mean you will do less work, just that you will feel better about yourself for having accomplished everything and then some.

- If you don't have a board, build one. Hold yourself accountable to a small group of people who have your best interests in mind but won't let you off the hook.

ASKING FOR HELP

Many entrepreneurs need to learn things themselves. Getting the advice of others isn't enough to warn them off a particular path.

If you're in this boat, you're in trouble. You will never have the time to experiment with everything. You need to pick and choose the times you take a new path.

No matter how much traction and success you're having, time and dollars are always at a premium.

Asking for help is life's best shortcut.

Those offering advice aren't always right, but their experience should help open your eyes to the challenges you'll face. While you'll be quick to dismiss suggestions because of the nuances of your business, seeing how the person offering that advice thinks through a problem is critical. Getting advice from others may not provide the right path, but it will provide the right criteria against which to evaluate your next move.

The only sure thing about a startup is that you need help. Whether that's advice from someone who has navigated your market before, an introduction, or someone to tell you to keep going. You need others. Find them and listen.

Advisors
Market, execution, industry, and product knowledge are areas where you need the expertise of others to challenge your assumptions.

Reaching out cold to others who have been through it before is surprisingly easy. When you show vulnerability and ask for the expertise of others, you get help more often than not.

Everyone has a bias toward their own areas of expertise and the formula that worked for them in the past, so identify a well-rounded group who can push your thinking in every functional area.

Customers
Asking for a recommendation or referral feels enormous but should be easy. The downside is minimal.

The worst that can happen is you hear 'no' and get a list of things that aren't working well. That's invaluable feedback. It makes your product better.

Other Entrepreneurs
Introductions to investors, vendors, or other collaborators are at your disposal. As are frameworks and stories about having faced down similar challenges.

If you're willing to reach out, most will be willing to help.

It's an area where they can give immediate feedback and recognition, both of which are often in short supply. And that value goes both ways.

Consider These Actions:

- Know your weaknesses. What thoughts make you feel uncomfortable? Admitting what you don't know is the first step to filling that gap.

- Mentally reframe what it means to ask for help. Admitting you don't know something is a strength, not a weakness. You're putting your company before yourself.

- Use your professional networks exhaustively. Wrap every conversation with an ask for help; new contacts, reviewing your efforts, etc. (But offer your help in return. Every. Single. Time. The more you give, the more you get.)

FINDING CONSTRUCTIVE FEEDBACK

Positive reinforcement is something everyone requires.

You often hear that being a CEO is a lonely job. It's not. What the job is, however, is bereft of recognition.

From Employees
Some employees will feel comfortable telling you that you're doing a great job, but it's rare. They are not that different from you. You probably don't remind them of the good work they're doing as much as you should either.

From the Board
Your board will focus on the thousand things that need improvement. They see their job as providing stewardship over the money invested. That means looking around corners and pushing the company to grow faster. What happened yesterday is already in the rear-view mirror.

From Yourself
Your inner voice is comparing the company to the best competitors in the space or the explosive unicorn the media loves. Worse, regardless of your traction, you'll go to bed each night thinking about the challenges that need to be addressed and further drive home the message that you're not doing enough.

From Your Spouse & Friends
This group is likely impressed and very proud of what you've accomplished, but it likely feels empty. You dismiss (or at least discount) it because you wouldn't expect to hear anything less from them.

There's a foil to every 'attaboy' you get. It's unfair, but that makes it no less true.

Instead, create a metric-driven scorecard. The scoreboard is always objective, and if you realize you need to score a point before you can score two, then you'll ease up on the 'well we're not at two points yet' thinking.

We humans need feedback loops. Take control and create your own so you aren't waiting for it from people who aren't likely to give it.

One mistake I made was basing the scorecard too much on revenue. Revenue is paramount, but it's too fickle and not wholly representative of the job you're doing. Instead look at the pieces over which you have more control— the effort that goes into generating revenue (new leads generated, product use rates etc.).

Without feedback loops, only your inner critic is left to judge. That critic is rarely constructive or forgiving.

Consider These Actions:

- Measure what's in your direct control. Measure frequently and physically plot it out. Things don't always go up and to the right but seeing the trends can help prevent you from beating yourself up too badly at each dip.

- Incorporate employee surveys to gauge enthusiasm, belief in the strategy, etc. Quantified metrics on a scale can be meaningful enough to make you feel better.

- Join a CEO group. YPO, Vistage, etc. are great opportunities to get objective feedback from those in similar shoes.

TALKING ABOUT YOUR COMPANY

Ask an entrepreneur how things are going and nine times out of ten the answer is bullshit.

There are a hundred things going wrong at any given moment.

When you're asked, don't reflexively say things are fantastic. It's (often) disingenuous, but it also closes the door from getting help. Understand the question is often asked because it's expected, but people rarely refuse when asked for help face-to-face.

This is an opportunity to flip your unease into something useful.

"Things are going reasonably well, but I could really use help doing [xyz]. Do you know anyone I should talk to about that?" That is a lot more meaningful for someone to lend a hand than, "Things are incredible. We just launched [xyz] feature." One leaves the door open, the other closes it.

Ask for a new perspective or alternative ideas to solve a problem. It's an opportunity to get that from someone who can empathize with the challenge and viscerally understands its import. That is rare.

It won't often progress you toward a goal, but in that odd occurrence it does, it's free value.

The 'fake it until you make it' mantra is doing entrepreneurs an enormous disservice. Incidents of depression are *three-times* more likely in entrepreneurs. By playing Little Mary Sunshine, you're not only missing out on an opportunity to expand your knowledge and network, but you're potentially exacerbating another entrepreneur's depression.

So, talk about things that aren't going as well as you'd like. Ask them for their opinions. It'll give them a chance to help and feel valuable. When you make others feel useful, they will want to come back to that well for another drink. This is an opportunity to build a support network to catch you when you're falling or, even better, throw you the parachute.

Consider These Actions:
- Give yourself permission to be thoughtful instead of prideful. You show more strength through weakness than you do through false bravado.

- Always know the help you need. Have an ask always at the ready. Part of the challenge is that we tend to reflexively answer questions— "Things are great." Try: Things are alright, but I could really use some help solving [xyz]. Have you faced that?"
- Build a coalition of the honest. Surround yourself with others who are willing to admit things aren't perfect, who aren't afraid to ask for help, and who are willing to give themselves to your cause.

SEEKING BALANCE AND FAILING

Work – Family – Yourself.

Finding the balance between the things you value is impossible because it doesn't exist. There are simply tradeoffs.

It's the quality, not the quantity of time that matters.

The key isn't balance, but *focus*.

Play in one bucket at a time. If you're thinking about work when you're spending time with the family, then you're not really spending time with the family.

When you're in family mode, be in family mode at full force. Your kids would rather have your undivided attention for two hours than compete with your phone all day.

If you're doing something that revitalizes you, don't let the task list creep into your mind or feel guilty for prioritizing your needs.

You will err on the side of over-working. Guaranteed. But you have diminishing returns that you are too close to see. After a certain period, you become horribly inefficient and wind up wasting your time just so you 'feel' like you're trying hard enough.

The imbalance I'd been living with struck me right between the eyes after getting kicked out of the company I founded. It was the most painful experience of my life. The company predated my children and I'd spent nearly every waking moment thinking about how to nurture it and help it grow into a model adult.

After the ejection, I found myself with a lot of time on my hands and a lot of pent up resentment. I channeled that into house projects. I kept my son home from pre-school a couple times a week so we could work on projects together.

We painted the house, built outdoor furniture, hauled juniper bushes to the dump, and drove a backhoe around.

For the first time, I truly saw him. He was four.

Even though I'd spent time with my children when I was running RoundPegg, I was rarely present. My mind was constantly making lists of what needed to get done or thinking through the latest challenge. My eyes were constantly focused on my phone and keeping up with e-mail.

It was an awakening to all that I'd missed by prioritizing the company as my first, second, and third priority.

Give yourself permission to take the time off. Shrug off the glorified tales of founders sleeping under their desks and working 100-hour weeks.

Creativity isn't linear and doesn't scale by simply thinking harder. It's like looking at a dim star. Sometimes you have to look away and keep it in the corner of your eye in order to actually see it.

You <u>can</u> take the time off to spend with your family. You <u>can</u> go exercise. Not only are you not as productive as you think when you work longer hours, but you are, in fact, adding stress and making your life harder. Stress releases cortisol in the brain. Cortisol inhibits creativity. If you're professionally searching for a still-unknown solution, then work is a creative pursuit. You're only making your job harder by thinking more intently.

Consider These Actions:
- Redefine what success looks like for work, family, and yourself. Be *reasonable*. You won't be perfect in any of the three, so don't expect it.
- Schedule time for non-work activities. Carve out explicit family time, exercise time, or sitting on a rock time. The key isn't the scheduling itself but giving yourself permission.
- Rate yourself at the end of the time block to evaluate how effective you were at focusing on your family, work, or yourself. It sounds antithetical to the idea of relaxing and focusing, but it will keep you honest.

ENCOUNTERING COMPETITION

The odds are that you'll be oblivious to others in your space when you get started. That ignorance is comforting. It keeps you going.

At some point, someone will forward an article about a company doing something similar. You'll feel like you've been kicked in the stomach.

But it's a positive. Really. The sooner you can see it as such, the faster you become better.

The concept behind RoundPegg was that employee performance was situational and that someone would perform better if they fit with the existing company and team culture. And what better way to figure this out than by testing candidates before they joined your ranks?

It turns out that I had invented something that had been around for 2,200 years. I didn't even know what phrases to search to decide if I had any competition. It was a lucky break since simply typing 'pre-employment tests' would have returned hundreds, if not thousands, of incumbents. Had I known, odds are that I'd never have taken the next step, figuring that the market was being served.

One specific encounter— and the resulting pit in my stomach— still sticks with me.

It was a 27-minute call where the guy completely crapped all over the idea— how hard it was, why it wouldn't work, and why the approach was wrong. I let that keep me down for a week until I realized this guy was struggling to survive and felt threatened. This was a good thing.

Even more, it highlighted that competition is needed.

Few people seek to be the first to buy within a brand-new market. Without competition, your prospects can't properly vet the field and make a long-term decision that's right for them.

With competition, you have a market. Competition educates your buyers, so you don't have to spend the time and the dime to do so. Competition will do good things which give you free ideas to 'borrow.' Embrace it.

Consider These Actions:

- Relax. Know that what you read about your competition's product is puffery. Know that the brands they list on their website are indeed likely customers, but in tiny pockets. (It's not hard to get a friend to try a product in order to acquire a logo.)

- Return to focusing on your company. You have a vision of what needs to be. Execute on that.

- Take their best ideas. Every company is doing one thing better than you. Whatever they're doing better, find it and execute it without their mistakes.

DECIDING AMONGST BAD OPTIONS

More than once, you'll face the choice of making a bad decision or shutting down the company. It's part of the startup process.

You have to make the *least* bad decision available.

The right decision is usually the one that buys yourself another day. Staying afloat that extra day gives you one more day to correct that least bad decision.

In the early days, <u>time is your revenue</u>. You do whatever you can to keep the doors open in order to give the team another chance to release a product or set up a demo. You need the opportunities to succeed that only come with time.

The decisions you make today are ones that you know you'll one day laugh at or be ridiculed by 'professional management' should they take over. Contracts from the early days are going to look atrocious to those who join the company later. It is what it is. The ideal option, the one you know you would and should choose, isn't available to you. When you're tiny, you have no leverage and are forced to cut deals that give you the slimmest glimpse of daylight.

Here's how I faced this: Though I was newly married, my wife and I hadn't yet combined bank accounts. Overdraft fees were within sight. My co-founder and I had to put a deadline on our fundraising process strictly for practical reasons. We needed to pay rent. We'd decided that if we hadn't come up with $250,000 by February 5th at 5 p.m., we were going to scrap the business and go get 'real' jobs.

I could cover March rent, so it'd give me seven weeks to find something new.

At 2 p.m. on the 5th, we got an e-mail committing $75,000, putting us $20,000 short of our goal. Close enough.

But the money had strings. We had to hire the investor and pay him a salary. He had no startup (from scratch) experience, no relevant industry experience, and very little emotional intelligence. There wasn't a whole lot to like about this deal other than the money to buy time.

It goes against everything any mentor will tell you and against the screaming voice in your head that knows the incentives are misaligned.

Our choice was to keep the business going or shut it down.

We kept going.

Things turned out as you'd imagine. Another voice in the mix made every decision take twice as long, strategic differences were exacerbated, and the effort was less than hoped. After four months, we couldn't justify it any longer.

We fired our investor.

If we could have bet the entire amount of capital we'd raised that it would lead to a negative outcome we would have. The options in front of us were terrible. But we did what gave us another year to figure it out. We made the least bad decision.

Consider These Actions:

- Write down your options and the likely results. Every decision has an associated time cost. When in doubt, pick the one that buys more time.
- Have the unfailing confidence that you are good enough, smart enough, and obstinate enough to recover from every knowingly bad decision.
- Share your decision-making process with the team. You're earning their trust with every decision, so it's critical they know what you faced when identifying the sub-optimal path as the best way forward. Give them the credit for knowing it's sub-optimal while also giving them the data to understand it's the best course of action.

CO-FOUNDERS

There is no overstating the importance of the relationship between the co-founders.

My first co-founder and I met when we literally bumped into one another in a coffee shop. We were trying to solve the same problem and had complimentary skills. It was a no-brainer to hitch our wagons together.

Our lack of history together, however, meant we didn't know what drove the other and what the actions were that shut the other down or made them feel slighted. We also didn't have the trust in one another to admit our own needs. While it seemed like fate, it ultimately ended as you may expect total strangers starting a company together would.

For the first five years, RoundPegg grew at a healthy clip - nearly doubling each year. Things were okay, but not great. We had just enough success to paper over our differences – strategically and interpersonally. Revenue kicked the can down the road because problems aren't problems if you aren't failing.

What we didn't recognize (or maybe just couldn't admit) was that we needed the same thing from the business. We were competing with one another for it.

He'd been in his prior co-founder's shadow for so long that he was desperate for external validation, just as I was after failing for the first time in my career.

What started as petty slights festered into a lack of respect over the years. Our competition for that external validation had us pushing one another down instead of hoisting up the other. It did nothing but hurt our business. It closed our minds to the other's ideas and made each day less fun than the day prior.

Our focus on one another blinded us from recognizing how we were closing deals. Instead of being a united voice in the process, our board pushed to hire a head of sales to resolve the debate. It was less effort than fighting, so we acquiesced. A year of flat revenue followed, and the skies let loose.

We were at a crossroads.

Both my co-founder and I were justified in our approaches. We'd each been able to sell what we saw as the path. If the two of us and the rest of the board had the ability to put personal feelings aside and objectively look at the data, the path was clear as day. But board alliances being what they were, made that impossible.

The board, knowing we had our differences, now demanded that we also hire a CEO. Money was already tight and yet we were being forced to spend more. Our problems compounded and it didn't work out for either of us founders, or the CEO.

The company sold for dimes on the dollar because we didn't put the work in upfront. By not admitting our needs and asking for help solving them, we took on (expensive) headcount that shortened our runway and took away our opportunities to recover from mistakes.

Worse, we compounded our mistakes by burning our shortened financial runway debating our go-to-market without the ability to hear one another. We torched what little time we had.

In the end, you and your co-founder are a team who have to work together for the good of the business. As often as you'll hear, "it's not personal, it's just business," that's 100% wrong. Everything is personal with co-founders because of the faith you must put in them. You have to know how to bring out one another's best, how to pick one another up through the tough times, and how to use one another for inspiration.

The more you know about one another now, the more you can dodge animosity later. And if you can find a way to share the scraps of validation that come along, you may be able to improve your outcome and the joy you get coming to the office.

KNOWING ONE ANOTHER'S NEEDS

Ego is not bad. Only ignoring it is.

Without your ego, you wouldn't have started something in the first place. You wouldn't have looked at the market and thought, "Yeah, I can do that better." Feeling guilty about satisfying your ego pulls you in multiple directions and creates friction between you, your co-founders, the investors, and your employees. You end up subverting others in order to get what you need, and they don't understand why.

Egos bring companies down. Not because they exist but because they go unfed and unrecognized. When we starve our ego, it will overcompensate in order to stay alive.

Admitting your ego's needs is not easy. It goes against everything polite society demands. But the only guarantee is that your ego will not be satisfied if your company fails. And failing to recognize it leads to failure. Period.

I wanted to be thought of as the 'smart guy' who connected information across disciplines and turned academic theories into life-affecting products.

I never admitted that. It seemed so self-serving. I thought I'd be putting my own needs ahead of the company's. I couldn't have been more wrong.

My failure to acknowledge that led to a massive crack in my relationship with my co-founder in our first year. At a TechStars 'Beers with Mentors' event, my co-founder and I introduced ourselves to a local investor. "Which one of you is the CEO?"

After my co-founder said it was him, the investor followed up with, "so this is all your idea?" A long, uncomfortable pause later, "yes, it is." Not only was it untrue, but it violated my ego's needs. Our relationship was never the same. I became overly sensitive to my ego being robbed of nourishment and hyper-aware of his need to be the 'smart guy' too.

Our needs overlapped. I couldn't vocalize mine and he couldn't recognize his.

Disaster.

Consider These Actions:

- Write your story. When all is said and done, what do you want the story of you and your company to be? Putting it in writing gives it a voice. Now you just have to read the words to your co-founder.

- Know your triggers. There will be things that get said or actions taken that will starve your ego and make you unproductively furious. Address those triggers with your co-founders early and often. Lead off your founder syncs with a rehash of both of your needs and whether they're being met.

- Write down your co-founders' needs and carry them with you in your wallet. Tape it to a credit card so you see it every time you buy something. You need to know his or her needs, so you don't trample them while trying to meet your own.

DIVIDING THE ACCOLADES

The effort that goes into getting the company off the ground is never recognized externally. Everyone is an overnight success as far as the media narrative goes. Even worse, they think it's because <u>one</u> of you is a genius.

The spotlight has a way of illuminating your internal differences.

Startups are often founded by a collection of equals. It's fair. It ensures everyone gives their all. But at some point, the need will arise to have a spokesperson.

The downsides of that position are that you travel far more, become distanced from the product and the team camaraderie, and you take the lumps when the negatives occur.

But it's an all-you-can-eat-buffet for the ego.

The recognition, no matter how much you include your team, is yours. You feel it firsthand. It can make others on the team resentful and reinforce their belief that you're seeking the spotlight for your personal brand rather than the company's. They will feel their contribution is being devalued.

The teams who survive these issues are the ones who are either comprised of extreme introverts who just want to focus on their domain or the ones who have discussed the implications ahead of time. Take the time to be the latter if you aren't the former.

Consider These Actions:

- Split the spotlight. Who owns which pieces of the business? Should something arise (PR, industry events, etc.), promote the one who owns the domain being featured.
- Create rules of engagement by knowing one another.
    - Who needs the spotlight?
    - Are there phrases that should be avoided (e.g. singular possessive pronouns)? Or repeated (e.g. Andrea, Company [xyz's] co-founder,)
    - What phrases should *always* describe the other? This is about branding the other in the way they desire.

- What areas of credit are granted to the other?
- Check in often and highlight specific examples of things your co-founder has done for which you're grateful. Recognize their success when the outside world may not.

DECIDING WHO GETS THE FINAL CALL

There is no hierarchy in the beginning. Titles are irrelevant and, while one of you may have the CEO title, it's entirely meaningless until you're large enough that you're no longer watering the plants.

What you do have though is a lot of work to do. You need to be able to trust your co-founder to work just as hard as you do. That requires you to acknowledge the areas where he or she knows much more than you do.

In some cases, this is easy. Often, the tech founder tends to shy away from closing the sale. Or the other knows nothing about writing code. But there are a ton of areas where it gets gray. Investor pitches, product features and priorities, marketing messaging.

It's easier to decide how you will interact with one another before there's ever any disagreement. One of you has to be on the hook for making the final call and 'breaking the tie.'

It need not always be the CEO. You are each good at something different. Leverage that and trust the other to make the right call.

More than decision-making and pacifying egos, knowing who breaks the tie allows you to play to your strengths. That's mandatory when you're the new entrant onto the market, going up against others who have the advantage of inertia.

Most important is finding a way to fund the company.

One of you will be better at making sales. Put that person 100% on selling. Sales is non-dilutive and helps prove to investors that there is a business underneath your presentation. Sales gets the fund-raising process going. Typically, you won't generate enough sales to bootstrap, so you'll have to both sell *and* fundraise.

While the person handling sales may be better at both sales and fundraising, you have to maximize the total contribution instead of maximizing each function.

For example, say you'd rate as an 8 of 10 on the sales side and a 7 of 10 on the fundraising side. Your co-founder is a 5 of 10 on both. You're better off with you on sales and your co-founder on fundraising (13 total points) than the reverse (12 points) or having you split your time on both (7.5 points, if you're lucky).

In my case, my co-founder and I briefly shared the CEO role. Though he was better on the product side and I was better going to market, neither of us could relinquish the other. Both of us had ego needs that required we feel the company was ours (singular).

The inability to have an owner for each role slowed us down, created confusion, and limited our success. Optimizing the whole sometimes requires being sub-optimal on a part. As a founder, until you come to grips with that and allow each other to make the final calls, you'll be operating sub-optimally everywhere.

Consider These Actions:

- Each of you make a list of where the other is stronger than you. Forcing yourself to see the positives in the other will help mitigate defensiveness.

- Agree upon which factors matter when making a final call. Does it meet short-term goals? Long-term? Does it fit the vision?

- Include aspects beyond the functions: Culture, incentive structures, how to hold meetings, etc.

- Change your mind. When presented with a good argument and things are equal, go with your co-founder's idea. You're not relinquishing your authority, you're gaining trust.

CREATING ACCOUNTABILITY

There's a lot that needs to get done. It can be overwhelming, even for those who are good at prioritizing.

Self-imposed deadlines will be missed time and again. There will be pieces of the business that don't get accomplished either because you've deprioritized them, they were harder than you originally thought, you forgot about them, or you just didn't feel like working on them.

These are the grains of sand that build into the pearl of frustration between co-founders.

Eschewing accountability is often borne from an entrepreneur's desire to not have a boss, knowing they can't fulfill their own commitments, or not wanting to demotivate or hurt their co-founder's feelings.

Regardless of the reason, accountability is important to make things feel real as well as to create infectious momentum. Accountability keeps one side from feeling like they're pulling more than their share of the weight. It also helps set the tone for what you expect from new employees when you get to that point.

There is nothing more frustrating than seeing the same bulleted item on the task list each week. It reinforces that negative soundtrack that tells you that you're not doing enough. It's not true, so you can't let it grow strong.

Consider These Actions:

- Commit small. With an endless task list, you'll always feel like you're not doing enough. Committing to just a few won't stop you from doing more, but it will gain your co-founder's trust that you will do what you say.

- Reframe accountability. Accountability isn't about punishment. Its purpose is to encourage action and build trust by fulfilling obligations. Like college football teams who get stickers on their helmets for great plays on the field, there is an office equivalent. Find it. Giant coffee mugs that get adorned with stickers for each week you nail your actions? Human nature is going prevent you from walking around with a stickerless coffee mug.

- Constantly reprioritize. If something didn't get done because it was less important than another thing, then ask if it's really important. If not, take it off the list. These aren't stone tablets.

PAPERING YOUR INVESTMENT

It's critical that any money you put into the company be treated just as any other investor's. You are not only an investor, you're the first one to take the risk. You should be rewarded for that.

Without legal documents detailing what you've financially put into the company, your investment will be, basically, stolen from you. When you raise money from investors, you're (typically) not in a position to make a lot of demands. There is no incentive for investors to negotiate against themselves and 'add' the tens or hundreds of thousands of dollars you contributed to the investment. It may seem like a rounding error when their percent of equity is counted, but they won't see it like that.

If you don't document your investment, it didn't exist.

This is critical should it ever come to slamming the doors on the company. As part of the first million invested, you can deduct it all from your income if the company goes to zero. It doesn't stop the pain of losing your baby, but it deadens the nerves slightly.

Consider These Actions:

- Have a convertible debt note drawn up for all the money you put in. Ensure the terms (interest and discount rate) are outlined or it is specified that you will accept the terms the investors receive when more than $X hundred–thousand dollars is raised. Most of these documents are boilerplate, so pay accordingly. Many accelerators will have templated documents available for download. Start there.

PLANNING FOR THE END

It's quite likely that your relationship with your founder will never be better than it is today. Use that to your advantage.

Neither of you are planning on leaving or kicking out the other, but the odds say that one of you won't be here when the company exits. Plan for it. You don't know which of you that will be or when it will occur. Use that ignorance to make a decision that's fair and reasonable.

Make it somewhat painful for the company to fire one of you. It's a protection mechanism from anyone who decides they know what's best for your company (your co-founder, 'seasoned' executives hired later, the board, your investors, etc.).

- Does stock vesting accelerate?
- Is there an option to sell a block of stock back to the company at the latest valuation?
- Is board-observer status guaranteed?

It need not follow a template. You can do anything you want now. Assume that anything out of the norm will be changed or renegotiated if and when institutional investors join the ranks. But everything can be negotiated. This is one more 'give' you have to give.

Consider These Actions:
- Plan the split when times are good. Draw up a founder's separation agreement that identifies terms so there isn't a negotiation over who gets what in the divorce during the acrimonious times.
- Deal with things openly. Most founders, even while bitter, still want what is best for their baby. If the board and the remaining co-founders encounter problems, discuss it openly before the drastic decision is made to cut one of you loose.
- Build in a safety net. For years, you and your co-founder have identified yourselves as your product or company. Finding another job isn't easy. Removing a little financial stress is sometimes enough to make it possible to more quickly move on and cheer (or at least not actively root against) from the sidelines.

TEAM

Buying the time to give yourself the chance to succeed is obvious when it comes to generating revenue and taking on investment. But the cheapest way to do it is through the people you hire.

Focus and the ability to say no minimize wasted time. Eliminating wasted effort quickly buys you full days to work on the things that matter.

In addition, providing recognition and customizing the work experience for everyone unlocks added effort that can propel you months or years ahead.

Neither are easy. The 'wasted' actions are never clearly labeled as such. And the added effort is hard to measure because it's often invisible, performed out of sight, like thinking through the company's challenges while they're in the shower or running on the treadmill.

Each require a bit of a leap of faith. But, frankly, you're an under-resourced company that's trying to catch up to more established competitors. There's really no harm in believing and focusing your efforts here.

The challenge is that it requires something different of you than what the company demanded when it was just you and your co-founder. As you add people, your role changes. You may still be an individual contributor, but you become more valuable keeping the team focused and moving in the same direction.

It's simple math. Many is greater than one.

The current model only faintly acknowledges that, however. The vocabulary of leadership is detrimental. The idea that you, as founder/CEO, 'lead' everyone implies you know all the answers. It suggests you are 'the decider' and are prepared to prescribe a team's actions.

People don't join startups because they want to punch the clock and do exactly what's asked of them. They opt into the unknown because they want to make a difference and undertake actions that they'd have no business performing in a larger, established company. They want to be heroes. They want to advance past the 'pay your dues' part of the career trajectory by proving themselves out of the gate. Let them.

That's a feature, not a bug.

Aside from making sure you don't run out of money; you won't make a larger impact on your business. Teamwork, motivation, and communication can be the most dominant competitive advantage there is.

But crafting that is squishy and feels like laziness. It requires meetings, one-on-ones, and walking around to collect information from everyone. It means acknowledging that the answers are not found in the glow of a computer screen but in the minds of your employees. We've been conditioned to think the former is work, while probing the latter is just socializing.

You need to give yourself permission to power down the computer in order to be effective in your new role.

In the marketplace, points aren't scored because of your ingenious idea or your inspirational speeches. The points are scored by players executing the plays better than the competition. Everyone must know what play is being run, what they're supposed to do, and what success looks like.

Everyone wants to do a good job. If you aren't convinced, think of how energized and ambitious people are in the first few weeks on the job. Most workplaces grind that out of them and then try to reenergize down the line with social events, competitions, and surveys.

Why not do things differently? Channeling their energy is a hell of a lot easier than creating that energy anew. 'Leading' is a function of understanding what drives your employees, what saps their motivation, and providing the feedback to keep them on the right track. It requires seeing the invisible and having the constant vigilance to put their needs at least on par (if not above) your own. It demands doing the not obvious work of channeling the employee's goals into something that will help the company.

As soon as you make the first hire, you start the transition from your role being one of pure brute force contributions anywhere and everywhere, to maximizing your return on your new investment.

Employees will be the largest line item on your P&L. If you're not going to let them run and seek the highest return on your investment in them, why hire them in the first place?

MANAGING YOUR TEMPERAMENT

Many entrepreneurs rely on their innate ability to surge on demand, to brute force 'make it happen.' But that rush of energy is not always useful when you're managing a team.

Having that tool at your disposal can cause frustration when others don't know how to wield it. It can make you emotionally volatile.

The more volatile your emotional swings, the more others have to manage to—and around—you.

As a leader, your role is to maximize the value your teams create. That demands creating focus on a challenge, the competition, and the customer. When others are forced to be wary of you, you become the focus.

The impact your emotions have on your employees is far, far greater than you can begin to imagine. Everything you say and do is interpreted—often misinterpreted—for meaning. The more unpredictable you are in your actions or the more volatile you are in your emotions, the more energy everyone has to invest in working around you. You are actively working against your own best interests by distracting your team from creating marketable value.

You're more effective when you can stay predictably medium.

The ability to acknowledge the realities—positive and negative—while maintaining a long-term view of what's best for the company, is one of the most valuable tools you can wield. It gives your employees the permission to stay focused on what's most important, rather than what you randomly deem urgent today. It creates focus on the things within your control, rather than reacting to the externalities of a lost account, positive media coverage, or the dwindling bank account.

If money is getting tight, figure it out.

If you're stuck raising a flat or down round, nobody cares.

You're going to look bad at the board meeting because you're missing sales numbers? That's your job.

Don't make your problems the problems of your employees. They have enough to do without managing your stress load, too.

Your temperament also dictates your ability to collect the one thing that's almost as valuable as revenue: information. Getting the whole truth about what's happening each day within your company is one of the most difficult parts of the job.

That information is under your team's control, not yours. You're at their mercy as to whether, how often, and how thorough that flow of information hits you.

Truth is only volunteered if you are consistent. If your team can count on you to process the information without 'shooting the messenger' and can anticipate your response, the more likely they will be to offer a version of reality coated with slightly less varnish.

That's not to suggest you can't get frustrated. You will absolutely be tempted to explode at missed deadlines, bad news, or poor decisions, but staying medium is often the best path to creating long-term effort and ideas.

There is a place to strategically use the emotionally fiery founder card. It will typically get results but played too often and you risk losing the team's dedication. They end up feeling like they're doing the work for you rather than for something bigger. Your temptation will be to get the near-term result and deal with the fallout later, but there's typically only one critical mountain to climb each year. You'll believe there are more, but hindsight will prove otherwise. Your job is to recognize which mountain is the one that matters every year.

If you must play the emotionally charged card, play it on that annual mountain alone. If you don't use it judiciously, you get a team that plays not to lose rather than to win.

Consider These Actions:

- Lead with questions. Ask what others would do first while you buy yourself a minute to quiet your inner, ugly reaction.
- Check your mood. Bring yourself up or down to find the center.
- Easier said than done in the moment but walking away (e.g. "let's talk about this later") or having a phrase to remind you that this is about the company, not you, helps to remove some heat.

- Keep your priorities and risks in your pocket (literally—on an index card). This will help you remember what's next and what can wound the company. When things are going really well, it will remind you of the job left to be done.

OWNING THE FIRST FIVE MINUTES

You're going to have bad days. You'll have mornings consumed by emotions emanating from losing a customer, getting cut off in traffic, or refereeing your kids fighting.

But you <u>must</u> leave it at the door.

Everyone feeds off you, and your mentality sets the tone for others. It's not fair, but it's reality. Your mood is enough to shift the daily dynamic and can have an outsized effect on the entire group's performance and creativity.

It's critical that you channel your energy into being constructive.

You set the tenor every day when you walk in the office. It doesn't mean you have to live in a fairy tale where everything turns to gold. But you absolutely can't be an angrier Eeyore.

Your negative energy will, often literally, scare your employees.

They'll avoid approaching you with an issue. They'll avoid offering suggestions on how to improve things. They'll avoid *you*. And that is the worst thing possible, because you're uniquely situated to have a view across the entire business that requires constant updates and ideas.

Your mood matters. Even if you have to fake it, find the positives. Just for five minutes.

The moment you enter the office, your team is looking at you for clues as to your mood. Are you approachable that day? Are you excited to be there?

The team won't mirror your feelings completely, but you will shift the compass a few degrees. Those few degrees could be the difference between generating a positive ROI for the day or just another day of burning cash.

Consider These Actions:
- Laugh. Before you get out of your car, laugh. You'll feel like a fool faking laughter, but it releases dopamine and will help improve your mood.
- Praise someone. It will help you recognize what is going well.

- Ask for help. The first person you run into will undoubtedly ask how you're doing. Tell them you're grumpy and ask them for some good news. Be enthusiastic about it and thank them for anything they give you.

AVOIDING EMOTIONAL WHIPSAWS

Things will feel out of your control, but you can help maintain balance.

Remember that game where you had to navigate a small metal ball through a maze by twisting two knobs that would tilt the board forward and back or side to side?

Leading your company is like that. Your workplace is the ball and it encompasses everything from people to strategy to competition to finances, etc.

When the board is stable and balanced, the ball is still or rolling slowly. It's easier to tip the ball in the direction you need it to go. If the ball picks up too much speed, you overreact in the opposite direction and it becomes nearly impossible to avoid the holes in the board.

That game is hard enough when you're the only one tilting the board. When you allow others to try to tip it simultaneously, chaos reigns.

It's okay—even good—to be scared of what's happening and what you can't control. But it's not okay to thrust that upon the team. They need to perform on the field, which means trusting the ball is rolling smoothly in the proper direction, trusting you to sidestep the holes, and trusting that their teammates are also focused on rounding the next corner.

Own the hyperventilation yourself. Alert everyone to the challenges with the confidence of clarity.

As a leader, your job is to keep everything balanced: pressure, energy, communication, focus, and relationships (and the list goes on). When you feel yourself getting pulled too deeply into a particular issue, it's likely due to an imbalance amongst the team.

- When teams feel too much pressure, they fail to see the obvious, creative solution. Too little and they don't anticipate the downside.

- When energy flags, you have people leaving at 4:55p and deadlines are missed. When there is too much, people burn themselves out.

- "Too much" communication (I hear your objection from here), everyone complains about being in too many meetings and not being able to get work done. Too little and everyone complains about not being part of the process.

- If everyone is too focused on solving one issue, it exposes a flank that competitors can exploit. Too little focus on the challenges and you may fail to anticipate the market's next move.

Make the list of things that are demanding too much of your attention and you'll start to see which of the knobs need turning to slow the ball down.

Consider These Actions:

- Know the score. Create a scorecard to measure the facets that matter most to your teams. For example, motivation, alignment, team dynamics, stress, focus, etc. Poll them.

- Anticipate how new projects and challenges will land given the current climate inside your four walls. Craft ways to raise the issue in a method that creates more focus rather than an all-hands-on-deck scramble.

- Reconnect with everyone individually to understand and address concerns. Ask them to play a role in keeping the balance.

- Repeat the mantras that remind everyone what you're solving and why you're in business. You can't repeat those things often enough.

CHANGING YOUR MIND

The ability to change your mind is an under-appreciated skill.

Modeling the behavior we want from our team is not rocket science, nor is it easy. One of the hardest things for anyone to do is to change their mind. Doing so implicitly admits that you were wrong. That's difficult. Doubly so when you're the 'boss.'

Changing your mind has a lot of positive benefits to your team. Namely:

- proving that the best ideas, not just your ideas, win;
- highlighting the importance of listening *and* comprehending what others say;
- valuing one another's solutions;
- underscoring that it's okay to be wrong—nobody has all the answers; and
- creating a safe place to throw out new ideas without repercussions if they don't work

You have a vision of what the world looks like when your company is dominant. You know every piece of the puzzle that must fall into place to get there. Thus, it's tempting to not just play air-traffic controller but to also tell every pilot how to fly their plane.

Changing your mind means being comfortable with a solution that you aren't absolutely convinced is the perfect solution. In the end, there are usually ten ways to solve most issues. Eight of which will probably work.

Further, most decisions are not major. The implementation of a new feature may seem big, but regardless of how it's implemented, it will need changing. Know that it will always be better the second time through regardless of whether your approach or theirs is taken first.

You'll forever be able to excuse away the fact your ideas are better because you think about the business non-stop, you've studied the market for years longer than your employees, or just because it's your company.

It's a trap.

While it may make sense to you, your employees feel unheard and unappreciated. People can only tolerate so much before they shut down and just follow orders. At that point, you'll get frustrated with their lack of initiative. No matter what they do (or don't), you will be frustrated.

So, choose the frustration that comes with the added benefit of engaged employees.

Consider These Actions:

- Start small. The major decisions aren't the time to practice this.
- Verbally acknowledge you're changing your mind. To model the behavior desired and to give your team ownership, you actually have to say, "You're right. Your idea is better."
- Try not to change your mind after a decision has been made and the team has started down the specific path. If it's bound to be a disaster, change course. If the outcome is unknown, sit tight and make micro adjustments as the team traverses the path.

REMOVING EXCUSES

Excuses are a symptom, not a disease. Excuses are offered up when an employee gets less out of the job than what they think they're putting into it (by their math).

It's not the excuse that is dangerous but the festering resentment behind it. When the employee making excuses goes to lunch with a co-worker or meets with others, their grievances are bound to be aired. Grievances are contagious and, even when not taken to heart by others, affect the quantity and quality of work. Engaged employees won't switch uniforms but they will get frustrated that the aggrieved employee's excuses are tolerated.

Excuses are a slippery slope to missed deadlines, poor performance, or failure to complete a task.

One of the more important components of your job is to facilitate execution. To do so you must get people to stop making excuses.

When you write your job description, carve time to be the utility player that will step into a hole and fill it for as long as needed. If you're willing to bend over backward to help others, take responsibility for missing deadlines, and be wrong, then you take away nearly every excuse.

If nothing is beneath you, then no role is beneath anyone.

If you put the team on your back to meet a goal you show that deadlines matter.

If you're the first to admit mistakes, everyone has permission to do the same.

If you're fielding an upset customer's complaint and accepting responsibility for letting them down, then nobody else can point fingers.

This is more than leading by example, it's strategically removing every possible excuse to ensure everyone focuses on the job at hand.

When there are different rules applied to you than to your employees, you're opening the Pandora's box of excuses.

Consider These Actions:

- Get involved. Ask what you can do to help meet the deadline.

- Get dirty. Periodically take the role nobody wants and complete it quickly and well.

- Assign tasks to yourself when wrapping and summarizing meetings. Follow through.

PLAYING TO WIN, NOT NOT TO LOSE

Failing fast has become managerial shorthand for getting employees to try new things without concern for the consequences. It's an admirable thought, but it's application often comes with big drawbacks.

Failing fast is still failing.

First, massive changes and improvements often require trying something that takes time. That defeats the idea of failing fast in its own right. Getting modest improvements are possible when you're failing fast. Getting a quick, exponential increase isn't common. The fail-fast mantra actually works against what it hopes to produce because you're slowly eking out improvements while opening the door for interpersonal criticism when things don't go right.

Second, the goal is actually to feel comfortable trying new things in order to play to win. Failing fast and having the safety to do things differently aren't the same thing. If you want your team to feel comfortable taking the chance to try something different, then it requires more than the approval to start something (what the mantra implies). It requires the full safety net, whereby you jump in to own the failure alongside the employee, the mechanisms by which it's obvious the experiment should end, and the push to tweak or try something again.

Third, it assumes answers are easy. Failing fast seeks the no-exercise weight loss plan. But you're trying to disrupt an industry and that requires more forethought, planning, and dedicated focus by everyone on the team to make a dent.

Most critically, failing fast is often uncoordinated and fails to recognize the interconnectedness of the entire process. Trying a new feature is great when everyone is in the know and can set the right expectations, support it, and get the feedback. Failing fast is often individualistic and the answer we get is usually inconclusive because we don't know how it would have gone with everyone else putting their weight behind it.

Failing fast has had its day. While the sentiment isn't wrong, it has been misapplied. It ignores the process and mindset behind its origins and is now often used by people and companies that want the upside of trying new things but don't have the risk tolerance to fail.

Focus on the process that leads to those exponential results, not just the approval to start. You want everyone to play unafraid. That's different than being willing to fail fast.

Consider These Actions:

- Have a plan beyond the result. Know what you're looking to accomplish and have a plan on how you'll test different approaches. Everyone has to know their role in those tests so you can draw actual conclusions.

- Preserve the mentality of failing fast by recognizing attempts to improve the efforts that went nowhere and owning those that didn't work.

- Focus the team on solving the hardest problems. Publicize them, seek input, encourage communication around solving them, and periodically incorporate them into daily meetings.

WORKING IN PARALLEL, FINDING VELOCITY

There's a thin line between confidence and deception. One of my co-founders used to say, 'startups are a grift.' I hated it. It didn't feel nuanced enough to say that founders are anything but con artists.

Which, in a sense, is true. It *is* about confidence. But it's the confidence to follow through on what you say you can do, even if you can't do it yet, rather than making empty promises in order to extract dollars from others.

Every entrepreneur feels the pressure of time and that they aren't moving quickly enough.

The only real way of solving this is to work in parallel, rather than sequentially.

Working in parallel requires you have trust in others and they in one another. It requires everyone be able to make solid estimates and complete the things to which they've committed. Easier said than done, but better to give a date way out in the future and be early than a date that's near and miss.

Trust is only built when personal commitments are hit.

Working in parallel has downsides. Sales will feel that product isn't working fast enough. Support will think bugs are being reprioritized in favor of the feature flavor of the month. Your product team will think sales is over-selling. Few will be happy because they are working without a net. One group is taking another's stated commitments to heart and publicizing them to customers. It can be uncomfortable when you're not used to it.

But if you're able to show everyone how their role fits into the big picture, why their estimates matter, and what commitments will be made based on those estimates, you can slowly paint the picture that this is about the team functioning, not about any individual. As everyone starts to do their part, the flywheel picks up speed without requiring just your singular Herculean effort to get it going.

Consider These Actions:
* Track personal commitments in the one-on-one. Help your team understand how bad they are at estimating and encourage them to be right 90% of the time. You'd rather they sandbag a time commitment and crush it than be aggressive and miss. Only the former builds trust with others.

Over-communicate the big picture. It's not enough to know what play to run; everyone needs to know the rationale for the types of plays being called. Reiterate the game plan every chance you get to help remind everyone that it's about the team beating the competition and that every individual plays a role in that.

- Track the frequency estimates and deadlines are met within the friendly confines of your one-on-one meetings. There is no easy way to get to 90% but knowing there is someone paying attention helps.

- When a product deadline is going to be missed, ask the product team to join those calls to break the news. It will make them thoroughly uncomfortable, but it will also help to build empathy, so they understand how painful it is to let down a customer.

OWNING FLAGGING PERFORMANCE

Your teams won't always be engaged. They won't always understand how the company's needs differ from their own desires.

Though it may truly be their problem, it's always yours.

When you assume responsibility for other's performance (or lack thereof) you're far more apt to find a solution. While you have the title and authority to point fingers, it's enormously unproductive. Nobody is motivated hearing that they are the issue. People are motivated when you understand that something is preventing them from doing their best and you help find a better path that allows them to do so.

When you point a finger, remember, three are pointed right back at you.

While meeting with a seasoned CEO, I asked what her biggest challenge was.

I knew the company was struggling to raise another round of funding, had just changed sales leadership, revamped their focus, and were thinking of letting a handful of people go. The problems were numerous and distracting so it wasn't a surprise to hear, 'the leadership team isn't engaged.'

What did surprise me, however, was the next sentence. "I keep asking them what their problem is and how I can help fix it."

Wait, what?!

The problem is yours. You are the CEO. Every problem is yours.

We talked about how she needed to reframe that discussion. Something more along the lines of, "I have a problem. I have the sense that your teams are struggling with the different pressures we're facing and are finding it hard to engage. What am I doing to exacerbate that? What should I be doing differently? How can I help you get your teams going?"

By labeling the problem as your own, you create an opportunity for others to be a hero and offer suggestions; many of which will fall upon them to fulfill. The goal is to find solutions. Blame feels satisfying but it makes no progress toward the goal.

Consider These Actions:

- Frame every problem as your problem. When you assume responsibility, others will want to help you when you struggle. It also creates a model of accountability which many will follow over time.

- Address often. Solve problems when they're small. It's a lot faster and a lot easier to solve small ones than large ones.

- Give others space to vent. Provide a safe time and place for that to happen together so that it doesn't happen in front of others. That space will ease pent up pressures enough to avoid harmful confrontations.

CELEBRATING SMALL TO BUILD MOMENTUM

Maintaining motivation requires acknowledging the progress made along the way.

But outcomes, especially in the early stages of a company, are not always in our control. Sometimes a pitcher throws the exact pitch in the exact location he wanted and, yet, the batter still hits it out of the park.

Celebrating small is the idea that you should celebrate the process, not the results. When your company is small and going up against larger, better resourced competitors you can do everything perfectly and still not win the customer. But that doesn't mean you failed. It just means you need to go do everything perfectly again with the next prospect. Over time, that perfect execution will pay off more often than not.

Even so, each of those unsuccessful outcomes saps your energy and dings your resilience. In order to keep going, you have to find ways to replenish both. That's more than just taking time out of the office but taking time to focus on the positives rather than repeatedly trying to smooth the rough edges of every corner of the business.

If you're in business, something is going right. It may not be much, but it's there.

It's okay to acknowledge you're doing some things well and to stop beating yourself up for a day or week or however long you need.

The same goes for your mentality toward your employees. Don't blindly ignore reality, but a constant focus on the negative is disheartening. Leading is not multiplication—two negatives don't make a positive.

For those on the frontlines of lead generation, celebrate the efforts made to generate a demo. Be consistent. If their goal is 100 phone calls and they nail it, celebrate, regardless of how many demos resulted. (Then fine tune if the demos aren't getting set.)

Celebrate the fact they are sharing information with one another about what's working to get people to return their calls or to reveal the budget and timing of a decision.

Celebrate improvements that people are making or the selflessness with which they're sharing their findings.

The idea is you want to celebrate small things that lead to success, in addition to the success at the end. The small things that are within an employee's (and your) control may not always lead to the right outcome but celebrating the process will lead to a repeat of the desired effort.

Breaking the tasks into pieces that are consistently achieved 90% of the time will help keep everyone focused on the process. The completion of small tasks forces everyone to keep breaking a story down until there is something they can complete in a couple of hours.

Take the extra time upfront to break things down into 'fun-sized' actions. Beyond the celebration, it's also psychological. It's more motivating to check the box having properly estimated completion time than going home with a big project partially completed weighing on you.

Consider These Actions:

- Help your teams create a way to measure the process. Mile markers ensure consistency and create achievable goals. Do something celebratory around them when they're executed.

- Look beyond the money. Keeping the doors open and the bills paid is your job, but solely allowing yourself to acknowledge you've done good work based upon revenue numbers will leave you ignoring three-quarters of your employees and provide some dark nights on the occasions when external factors created misses.

- Use the wins to stay positive. It's too easy to get down when things aren't clicking, but there's a reason Piglet was the real leader, not Eeyore. Your employees want the optimistic wisdom of Piglet.

CREATING WE

Your relationship with every employee is unique. You aren't the same with one person as you are with the next. You'll like one more, you'll trust one more, or you'll find one more energizing.

Similarly, everyone needs something a bit different from you. A different style of communicating or different outcomes based upon your interaction.

While there's personal satisfaction in all of these relationships, the utilitarian need is to drive performance. The more people trust you to do what you say, to keep their concerns safe, to react consistently, and to reward their efforts, the more effort they will give.

Building that trust is like building your bank account. To accumulate effort, your actions need to make more trust deposits than withdrawals.

Every action you take makes either a deposit or a withdrawal from your employees' effort bank. Manage your account wisely.

Every move you make is watched. Your team *is* keeping score.

They want to know where they stand.

Each time you keep your word, each time you have a team member's back, and each time you put your trust in them to accomplish something, you make a small deposit into their trust bank.

When you deflect blame or look out for yourself before a team member, you're making a withdrawal. Unfortunately, the trust bank is a lot like an IRA. Withdrawals come with a tremendous penalty.

This isn't to say you need to be touchy-feely and overly emotional with your team. Just consistent and empathetic. You will still let rip every once in a while. Those sometimes have utility and can remind everyone that you're in business to be a business but know that withdrawal will require months of deposits to compensate.

The 'founder explosion' card should be used incredibly sparingly. Its overuse creates a callous whereby most will ignore your rantings. While there are some short-term benefits, those rantings expose the us vs. 'them' (or you) divide. Repairing it requires far more deposits than you may have the time to fund.

Consider These Actions:

- Be the bomb squad. Diffuse, don't explode. Do your best to avoid reacting to tough situations in real time. The best skill to possess is the ability to say, 'let's pick this up later,' and walk away. Give yourself time to put everything into perspective. If it's still worth a strong reaction, give it, but the value of time and perspective allows you to focus on consequences rather than personal actions.

- Be accessible. Treat the work of others as more important than your own. Set the expectations of how people can reach you for feedback/approval/task assignment and when you'll get back. Even a single word reply will suffice. Failing to respond sends the signal that their job is not important.

- Be consistent, but unexpected with recognition. People need to have a good sense of how you'll react to something in order to put themselves out there with new ideas, to admit mistakes, or ask for help. Your consistency is critical to make the minor deposits. At the same time, for the big lump sum, you need to show unexpected thoughtfulness and reaffirm the employee's value.

EVOLVING YOUR ROLE

Many founders are good at most things. It's why you're a founder. You've been able to connect dots others may not notice because you are cognizant of how the different functions operate. It provides you with the ability to advance the ball in multiple areas without the help of others.

But as the team grows, your role changes. You need to go beyond being a doer to being an enabler. Could you get things done better and faster than whomever is responsible for the task currently? Possibly. Probably.

But is that the best use of your time? Unlikely. Your mind is better spent thinking through the macro challenges (e.g. how to counter a competitor's price change) than on discrete challenges where others have experience (e.g. user design).

The larger the team the more valuable you become as a strategic thinker.

Your role needs to evolve from Quarterback to Offensive Coordinator. Rather than making things happen on each play, you pull back and call the plays. The coordinator ensures everyone is in the right position and knows where they are expected to be. Then you back away and hope the play is executed as planned.

Beyond seeing the next strategic move, by virtue of knowing how to do most things, you're in a position to make everyone more efficient. You understand a role's requirements and how it fits the big picture, enabling you to cut wasted effort. Shaving an hour per week for someone adds up. That hour accumulates to an extra work week every year.

Making a team more efficient in total is far more valuable than completing the next task better and faster. Five, ten, or twenty people will outperform one, no matter how good that one is.

Consider These Actions:
- Transparently communicate what you're working on and what your role is. Get feedback on your role to ensure you're doing everything that is expected of you.
- Be involved and course correct mid-stream. Not being responsible for tasks doesn't mean you're not involved. Working with your team throughout shows you're on their team instead of simply criticizing in the end.

- Lead with questions. It's the best way to coach others on how you want them to think through the tasks they must accomplish. It exposes areas that need improvement without providing judgment and potentially demotivating.

- See the section, *Gaining Time by Optimizing Jobs,* for suggestions to find efficiencies.

MAINTAINING CONNECTION AND FOCUS

Leading teams requires comfortable shoes.

You may think you're not interfering. But if you're hunkered down in your office, you're missing out on easy wins that can keep a company engaged, focused, and headed in the right direction.

Walking around and interacting with everyone gives you advantages that your larger competitors can't mirror. Specifically, the ability to:

Maintain Positivity & Productivity
People need reassurance. Constantly.

They need to know that their contribution is valuable, is valued, and needed tomorrow. The half-life of any feedback and reassurance is brief.

Checking in implicitly let's others know that they are working on the right things and reminding them why it's important. Their being able to read your body language and hear your voice when you tie the feature request to a customer makes it real. Your authenticity will shine and remind them that deadlines aren't artificial or that effort won't go unappreciated.

People want to know they are critical and it's far easier to verbalize it every couple of days than it is to increase their salary every quarter.

Your voice alone is worth thousands per employee per year. The amount you save by walking around is never found in financial statements.

Minimize Negative Conflict
If 70% of language is non-verbal, it's pretty hard to see the big picture if you're only reading and hearing.

You may not consciously acknowledge it, but only by walking around can you observe how teams are interacting within themselves and with other teams. Knowing what tension is bubbling allows you to turn down the heat before it boils over.

Improve Strategic Decision-Making
So much of your direction is the result of feedback from customers—the challenges they face, the features they want, and the price they're willing to

pay. But often, the answer isn't obvious. It requires mashing up ideas that you've heard from disparate corners of the office, connecting dots that may not know about one another, and seeing risks that are only now on the very periphery of the radar.

Walking around provides you the benefit of an unscripted conversation.

You will pick up on things that your employees won't. Not because they're not smart enough or strategic enough, but because they don't have access to the entire puzzle like you do.

Reiterate What Matters & Focus Effort
Last, it helps you be effective at the hardest part of the job—communicating consistently. Be it the mission or how we want others to work, we all have our mantras. This is an obvious opportunity to reiterate them in context of a single individual's job. It becomes more meaningful.

Your presence is more powerful than you realize. Walking around only amplifies it.

Consider These Actions:
- Ask open-ended, personal questions. "How are you doing?" "What do you need?" Occasionally arrive early or stay late so you catch employees when there are fewer people listening in on the conversation.
- Don't lose sight of individual dynamics within group settings. Pay attention to who speaks, the body language of those who don't, and the interpersonal dynamics within the group setting. Use that information to focus on who to check in with next.
- Keep track. If you pick up something valuable in a conversation, track it so you can revisit it later (e.g. a vicious bug or personal challenge) with the same person.

MANAGING THE INNER CIRCLE

Everyone wants to be on the inside; to be trusted and to be your go-to resource.

But there just isn't enough oxygen in any room to accommodate everyone. You're going to wind up with high performers to whom you turn time and time again. It's natural. You know they can achieve the task set forth well and without your oversight.

You must load balance though. Utilizing your stars makes short-term sense but does little to keep the remainder of your team motivated and executing.

Everyone on the team knows who the stars are. They understand that those people will get the plum assignments and responsibilities and will likely be privy to information they may not. They can tolerate a slightly tilted scale.

What doesn't sit well is when you blindly put your thumb on the scales and fail to recognize how unbalanced things have become.

To get everyone's best, you sometimes have to look for who can do a job well, not always spectacularly.

The task may be done better by the high performer and you may need to invest time throughout the process, but in the long run you'll come out ahead. Downstream you won't have to spend nearly the amount of time course correcting to get the non-stars head's back in the game. You won't have to spend the time to reassure and reestablish the trust with the other team members. And you may not have to invest in a lengthy hiring process should those people leave.

You're spending time up front to save it in the end. It will also help you gain confidence in more than just a single team member. And the more firepower you have, the better equipped you'll be to fight off the competition.

Consider These Actions:
- Maintain a scouting report on each employee. Keeping a physical list of the strengths of each team member will help you distribute workloads so even the non-stars feel their importance.

- Use your periodic engagement surveys to spot those who feel they're on the outside looking in early, before they become irreconcilable issues.
- Track the one-off assignments. The purpose is not just to balance the allocation, but to also highlight the good work everyone has done on a regular basis.

LETTING OTHERS FAIL

Of course, you could do it better. But that doesn't mean you should.

It's possible to hand off responsibility and still drive from the backseat. You need your people to own pieces of the business because you can't do everything. The more you let them take on, the more invested they'll become, and the greater return on your investment in the long run.

Given the demands on our time, allowing your team to come to their own conclusions feels like a luxury rather than a need. It's true in the short run, but over time, they'll learn more and you'll be able to offload more onto them which will buy you more time.

You probably know the 'right' answer. Or, at least, have a bead on one of the better ones.

One of the more difficult parts of managing is holding that back and leading the team to find the right answer for themselves. There are myriad reasons not to so. They may not get there, it may take too long, there may be other fires demanding attention, etc.

If you opt to own everything, it caps executional velocity, diminishes the effort others put toward the company, and degrades the quality of the solutions they provide. In a market where you're dancing with elephants, you're quick or you're dead.

Giving others the room to fail tells them a story that your words never will. It shows them you expect them to own their area of the company and that you trust them to do so.

The personnel benefits of doing so are three-fold.

1. It will keep good people around longer and it will take more money to lure those employees away if freedom is a part of your compensation package.
2. It focuses your team on what the solution means to your customers instead of what it means to you.
3. Your team learns faster by doing than by watching from the sidelines.

This doesn't absolve you of responsibility or necessarily free up your time. Your role is to still help prevent the team from failing by identifying the gaps and forcing them to solve the inevitable problem you see before they create it.

But sometimes you have to allow others to make their own mistakes, so they'll be more open to others' ideas the next time or two around. Odds are also that they won't make the same mistake again. When people climb out of the holes they dug, they begin to see the value of avoiding them in the first place.

Of course, if they don't learn, it's likely time to move on from one another. The sooner you know that the better.

Start by posing the challenge and the desired outcome. The discussion can then get kicked off with a question to get them thinking down the path you desire or by eliminating the easy, obvious answer that isn't truly a solution.

From there, you can probe how the suggestions would affect them in their day-to-day jobs. This often rules out another chunk of 'easy' solutions and opens their minds to how decisions trickle down to their daily efforts.

Ultimately, the team will agree, at least directionally, on a path ahead. You may find new ideas you hadn't considered or get talked out of a solution because of how it translates to your team's daily job. But in the end, everyone will come away thinking more holistically about the company and be more prepared to find solutions down the line.

Consider These Actions:

- Let go. Your solution may be better, but it won't be perfect. Know that you will create more value working on something else and give yourself permission to accept that trade-off.
- Proceed with the confidence that the difference between an A output and a B or C output will be repaid manifold by the employee you let tackle the important project.
- Be Socratic. Challenge the employees to back up their rationale and expectations via questions that lead them to your concerns and objections without your specifically stating them. This requires being prepared and getting their thinking ahead of time, so you aren't winging it or acting on emotion.
- Ask for alternatives. What did they consider that they didn't do? Why? If no others were considered, why not? If they had to craft alternatives now, what would they be?

SHARING BAD NEWS

One day, you'll feel the urge to suppress or sugar coat bad news. It won't work. It never does. Worse, doing so lessens your credibility and delays your real job; helping your employees manage past the news.

How people respond to that news is up to you. You can only control the discourse and allay fears when you're the messenger and when you've given forethought to the affect the news will have on everyone.

Often, it's the delivery, rather than the content, that incites a negative reaction. Sometimes a turd is a turd and if you refuse to acknowledge that with the hope of pulling one over on the teams, then you've either done a terrible job of hiring intelligent people or they are going to think you're a self-interested phony who can't be trusted to tell them the truth going forward.

Be the Messenger
Withholding information breeds distrust. Distrust will turn every borderline issue into ones that require your time and attention.

Reality is never as bad as what imaginative brains can create. You've hired smart people and those synapses will be working overtime to find the 'real' meaning in what you've delivered.

Further, withholding information ensures productivity is near zero, stress is at a maximum, and that stronger performers consider looking at other opportunities.

Control the Narrative
When you've thought about the effects on others, you can begin to allay fears as they first arise. If you have a response ready, it should help nip the kernel of concern before it becomes a full-fledged fear.

You have to stop thinking about how the news affects the business and how it affects people in their roles. Think narrowly about what it means for the next little bit, but also the long-term potential of their careers. You want to think like an employee in order to message it properly.

Have a Plan

End negative messages with a loose plan on how to address it and come out stronger. This is just as important to shaping the resulting narrative employees tell one another as delivering the initial communication itself.

You need not be right, and everyone will poke holes in the approach you provide, but it's a signal to the team that you're not willfully blind to the challenges ahead. Determination and pragmatism will beat phony cheerleading every day of the week.

Consider These Actions:

- Give bad news early. The only way you can be assured of being the messenger is if you spread the news earlier than you're comfortable. If you're comfortable, you're late.

- Acknowledge the negative. You're only believable when you are able to acknowledge that a turd is a turd.

- Focus on the individual. Everyone will hear it differently and react accordingly. The only way you can help people react constructively is if you hear their individual concerns. Approach them to hear them out. Most won't come to you.

HIRING TEAMS NOT ROLES

We're constantly on the lookout for the 10x employee. I'm sure they exist, but your likelihood of finding one is about the same as your unicorn exit. Yet we all believe. That mentality leads us to search for the most knowledgeable, most talented candidate.

Except we work in teams.

In teams, success is rarely driven by the brilliance of one person's idea, but the ability to get others to see the value in it, build it, and support it.

It's a cliché that teams are only as strong as the weakest link, but there's a lot of research showing this to be true. Research has proven that a team with a single bad apple suffers a 30-40% decline in group performance.

It's easy to think of a new hire as just one new body. But the reality is they work with others. Teams, on average, are a shade under six people strong. Thus, that one person creates hundreds of new communication dynamics just within the local team.

One person has a major impact.

We tend to overlook that fact because the upside is measurable and easily seen while the downside is just felt. Our bias is to optimize the known and attribute blame for the invisible elsewhere.

The downside of bad apples is measured in turnover, your time, and the opportunity costs of discord, missed goals, and pessimism.

Hiring is never easy. We just don't spend enough time with candidates to get a clear picture of who they are, how they work, and what their hang-ups are. There's value in selecting the interpersonally safe choice that mitigates risk rather than excusing away the small idiosyncrasies you noticed throughout the process in hopes of landing a "ninja/rockstar/guru."

Consider These Actions:
*   Make the interview process resemble the job. Every job has its pressure points or requirements that aren't necessarily fun or rewarding to do. Test for those as part of the process. For example, when hiring salespeople, provide a deadline on which why should hear back from you and then sit

on your hands for an extra week. The core function of the sales job is to follow up on prospects and hold them to deadlines they set. If the candidate doesn't get in touch and harass you, then they've shown they can't do that for your prospects.

- Ask candidates about how they work and what brings out their best/worst. Ask about the worst place they've ever worked and what made it so bad. Ask about the best boss they've ever had and what made her or him so great. The more you find out about what makes them tick, the better you can slot them into the team and bring out their best.

- When sending them the job offer, highlight the areas where you see differences between how that applicant, and the bulk of the team, work. Express your concern, while reiterating your belief in them if they think they can manage that difference. You've put the ball in their court. If and when the issues arise, they'll be slightly more ready.

HIRING COMPLEMENTARY INDIVIDUALS

It's rarely the case that an entire team is hired all at once. We hire one person at a time. Thus, we almost always fall into the trap of thinking about who the best person for the open role is rather than who the best person for the team is.

Your job is not to make great hires, but to build great teams.

Today, more than ever, the lone wolf is an endangered species. Very few roles fully operate independently without input, collaboration, or approval from others. Even in the instances when we can complete a challenge single-handedly, it's still critical others understand what we did and why we did it. Odds are that others will have to jump in to fix or improve things down the line.

Prior to making the hire for the next open role, you have to know the team's current dynamics, not just in terms of skill, but also mentality. What is missing? What is not working? What do they do really well?

Long-term, team construction is the most important thing that you will do as a founder. Yet, it's something nearly every founder, board, and investor deprioritizes.

New hires are often viewed as individuals who have a set of tools they can bring to the job. The skills and abilities have to complement the rest of the team, but the planning around team composition tends to end there.

The skills are only about what the team is capable of doing. The rest of the aforementioned intangibles dictate how closely the team comes to reaching (or exceeding) the individual capabilities.

You will hear a lot of theories about wanting a mix of introverts and extroverts, risk-takers and risk-avoiders, or methodical thinkers and reactionaries. But that overcomplicates things because very few managers are skilled enough to consistently manage the interpersonal differences on their team.

Mixing personality differences is theoretically sound, practically disastrous.

Unrecognized differences allow conflict to blossom. All of the downside, none of the benefits.

Unmanaged conflict becomes personal. Conflict amongst personalities creates barriers, at best, and sabotaging, destructive behavior, at worst.

The personal attributes you seek should revolve around how work gets completed.

If good and fast were opposite poles, where along the continuum would you want your company? How much are decisions discussed? If one pole is a group discussion and the other is mandated by you, where are you? How about how that decision is made? Is it the best answer or the one with which everyone is satisfied? What gets recognized and rewarded? How are rewards granted?

We all lie somewhere along a continuum. And the decision of where you hope the team will lie on the continuum isn't about finding individuals who match up to that point but finding people who cluster *around* that point.

Where the team ultimately lies requires more than just averaging what you have. If you have two people on opposite poles, you're not going to have a team that functions in the middle. You're more likely to have chaos and intractable opinions.

Instead, you'd rather have someone who skews slightly more toward risk-taking while one skews slightly less. Extremes can't see cases where the other position may be better. Those who skew are far more likely to have the capacity to see the other perspective. Their normal distribution, while skewed toward one pole, is much more likely to overlap with your desired position and the position of their opposite-skewing teammate.

Ultimately, none of it matters if you can't manage it.

We project manage features to death but rarely do so with the interactions required to get those features built. Hiring individuals requires understanding the machine in place.

You're working with invisible and imperfect information. Simply recognizing that and consciously accounting for a new hire's role within a team won't solve the challenge, but it will dramatically improve your success rate.

Consider These Actions:
- Analyze the team. Determine how you want the team to interact. Within everyone's one-on-one meeting with you, dig deep. Ask others what qualities they think a new hire should have and what their deal-breakers

are. They may not be right or relevant, but you'll know enough to address their concerns later.

- Get directed team feedback. The team is likely terrible at interviewing and will default to skills and common interests. You need their feedback regardless but give them the tools to dig into whether the workstyle will jive with what already exists.

- Arm the team. Give them questions to ask and areas on which to probe that draw out the applicant's prior experiences and behaviors.

FIRING EARLY EMPLOYEES

Many job descriptions include a quip about 'joining the family.' Early-stage companies have the benefit of added camaraderie, like recruits going through boot camp together, but it's a team, not a family.

You can't fire family members. You *can* fire team members. The goal of teams is to win. The goal of families is to love and support one another.

The difference isn't semantics, but one of permission and focus. You have to ensure the focus is on everyone performing at their best and running the designed play. If they aren't, you have to give yourself the permission to do what's best for the company and make the change.

Removing employees is never easy, and loyalty and historical performances should never be dismissed. But for many early-stage employees, they can become a net negative if they feel they're no longer in the inner circle.

Not everyone is right for every stage.

As the company grows and can afford to hire both more and more-skilled employees, the early employees will see their roles refocused into what they do best. For some, that feels like a demotion and that they're not being trusted, valued, or respected. Some can become rooted in how the company has worked historically and make your attempts to adjust to the new realities much more difficult.

The only antidote to growing the team and shifting the inner circle is transparent conversation.

If the conversations with these employees don't lead to their help driving the company forward, you need the mental flexibility to do what's best for the company and to find a replacement who allows you to focus on the whole, rather than just the parts.

Some people don't have the mental agility to make the transition. Be forthright with what you need and, if the mentality isn't changing, be quick to make a move. Quick can be both considerate and provide a soft landing (in fact it should), but even though that employee may have been vital to the success to date, you owe it to the rest of the team to make a change.

When the option is losing to the competition and needing to cut your workforce versus blind loyalty, the choice is obvious.

(Please don't mistake this with permission to be an unfeeling utilitarian. Make every effort possible to help adjust the employees' focus and how they define their value. But you can't afford to retain a would-be malcontent should they prove unwilling to redefine themselves.)

Consider These Actions:

- Push everyone to do their next job today. To stay in the inner circle and be part of the 'rising tide raising all boats,' they need to both expand their responsibilities and improve their skillsets.

- Be open and honest. Present the scenario to the early employee about what it takes to be great in the next role. Help them get there but be open about the company not having the time to wait for them to exhibit the skills and mentality if they don't show them first.

- Hire transparently. Involve the early employees in the hiring of new executives. The early employees know how the heart beats better than anyone and can be an incredible cultural filter for all hires. It may be awkward for them to hire their boss, but it's better for both parties in the long run.

DECODING DEPARTING EMPLOYEES

Once you hire your first employee, you're just counting down the time until you have a conversation where someone says they're going somewhere else for more money.

Money for time has always been the agreement. It's the cleanest and easiest one to provide. And when average tenures are measured in months rather than decades, the justification to invest emotional energy into employees becomes harder to make.

When people depart and cite monetary factors, the odds are that it isn't the money. Or at least not the primary one. Something got them looking in the first place. Assuming they were making a reasonable wage, there was something they weren't getting from you or from their job.

If they aren't seeing outward signs of your respect and recognition of their value, money becomes the default. When money becomes the employee's barometer, you will lose to better resourced competitors.

I'm not advocating paying people less than they're worth, rather to stop throwing good money at a problem created by a lack of respect rather than a lack of dollars. Your attention saves money.

Consider These Actions:
- It may sound financially sub-optimal but leveling pay from day one is the easiest starting point to ensuring fair compensation in the future. Monetary compensation is often locally relative. When given the choice, many people pick being paid the highest of everyone on the team rather than at the bottom of the team but near the top of the industry.
  - *Note:* You still want to negotiate salaries, but some will be less aggressive and 'earn' a lower amount. Gain early goodwill and credit for providing a 'raise' by leveling them up to meet their peers shortly after their start.
- Know the non-monetary forms of rewards that others seek. Whether it's a personal thank you, public recognition, or a new assignment, it will be cheaper than trying to compete with deep pocketed competitors in your industry.
- Consider being moderately transparent with your financials. If everyone knows where the company stands, it makes it more difficult for them, on

their worst days, to mentally make the silent argument that they are getting screwed by the company. In those dark times, there is all this money flowing in and they don't see where it goes. They assume the worst – that you're reaping the rewards of their hard work.

AVOIDING FINGER POINTING

Few people really understand the difficulties of another's job.

For example, closing a sale looks easy from the outside. You just have to talk about this great product and send a contract over. Most fail to understand that every deal is different, how often a salesperson is at the mercy of another's timeline, and how little correlation there is between showing up and closing a deal.

Similarly, the interconnectedness of a product's features is typically unknown to those who have never written any code. That you can't just copy and paste functionality from one place is mystifying. It's easy enough to do in the programs they use after all.

The commonality is a lack of understanding. That lack of understanding creates an empathy gulf which seeds internal strife.

When you bridge that gulf, you reduce the frequency of the interpersonal issues many times over because ultimately, people are looking for solutions, not just scapegoats. You also help build the fortress walls that ensure the outside world doesn't experience the chaos of your reality.

Getting people to work together requires everyone to understand all the tedious, unglamorous tasks that go into the results that get rewarded.

The best way to bridge this gap, I've found, is to get everyone to open up about the good, the bad, and the ugly of their jobs.

When everyone can admit that everything isn't ideal, they're opening themselves up for help. When people see others struggling, it's human nature to offer help. Nobody wants to see pain. Your teammates will rally around one another when you pave the way for them to both offer and take the helping hand. The simple task of asking for help shows vulnerability. It takes a particularly calloused individual to walk away from a willingly vulnerable teammate.

Approach interpersonal conflict from the belief that everyone wants to do great work and look good in front of their peers. We all know that if it were as easy as copy/pasting or just trying a little harder, those things would be done. Yet, in the heat of the moment, we rarely recognize that unless we hear from others about what it actually takes to close that deal or create that functionality.

Consider These Actions:

- Open up. At your next offsite, have everyone put together the list of:
    - What's the hardest part of their job?
    - When do they feel they're most exposed (e.g. when a customer asks when a bug fix will be completed)?
    - What can others do to help them feel less exposed or to make their job easier?
    - What do they wish they could do to help others?
- Remind often. When you convene all the teams, ensure everyone asks for help even if their goals have been hit. We can all use help, but it's a hard ask. Vulnerability leads to cooperation.
- Work with teams to offer up their assistance when they hear another team misses a goal. They should feel safe to say, "I'm sorry, I should have helped by doing [xyz]. How can I get more involved to help next?"

CREATING TEAM ACCOUNTABILITY

As a founder, you may find yourself frustrated that employees are not holding themselves to the bar against which you hold yourself.

It's code for, 'people aren't working around the clock like I did when I got this off the ground.'

Wanting your employees to 'act more like owners' or to 'hold themselves accountable' is like wishing for more revenue. It'd be wonderful if it happens, but it takes a lot more than wishing to make it so.

When you find yourself wishing for these things, it starts a destructive loop where nothing, but animosity is fostered. You hold it against them that they aren't working as you'd like and thus give less of yourself to them and are more likely to criticize than compliment. Those actions create the incentive for the employee to double down on the behaviors you don't want to see.

So, how do you stoke accountability?

The unthinking approach to getting everyone to act like owners is through stock options or hanging a sign on the wall that lists 'accountability' as a cultural value.

Neither work.

Employee's know stock options are lottery tickets. Nobody plays the lottery for a living.

That their equity is a small fraction of your own and at a price hundreds of times higher. The idea of equity is often better than the reality of it. That becomes clear the first time the company stalls and a 'difficult' round of funding looms.

Similarly, the words you put on your wall as your cultural values are completely meaningless until you start living, rewarding, and policing them.

Instead, focus on the leeway people have to get things accomplished. If they see an opportunity, can they pursue it? Will they be punished if it fails?

'Acting like an owner' is only possible if people are occasionally given the leniency to pursue a solution they see. That is, people act like owners when they are treated as such.

The converse is true of accountability. While the leeway you provide for people to do their jobs helps push them toward acting like owners, it's only your inattention that leads to a lack of accountability.

If people aren't following through on the things they say they're going to do, you have to start looking in the mirror. Do you follow through on the commitments you make to them?

Holding people accountable should be done in private. Teams are held accountable by holding the person in charge accountable... in private. You will learn things in private that won't be admitted publicly.

Consider These Actions:

- Get commitments. Have everyone pick one problem they are going to solve each quarter.

- Keep tabs. Know who has committed to what and keep them honest in their one-on-ones. Remind them that they set the deadline, not you, and that others count on things getting done when they say they are.

- Set expectations. The goal should be completing tasks when you say rather than speed. The goal is to build trust and confidence. It's follow-through and consistency, not speed, that achieves that.

- Set goals that can be hit 90% of the time. It builds the muscle that expects results rather than the muscle that spits excuses. Low bars create momentum, not low expectations. The people you hire are not the kind who will take half the week off if they reach a goal by Wednesday. Trust them.

BUILDING TRUST BY HITTING GOALS

Goals need to be coordinated like a dance. If a goal goes unmet, it has downstream effects on people in other functions.

Trust allows you to coordinate the dance. When you trust others, it flows throughout the company.

Trust provides massive economic benefits, from increasing win percentages and executional velocity to reducing customer churn and employee turnover. It allows everyone to work a little bit further out over their ski tips because they believe others will be there to help create the reality.

It requires developers and support to trust the sales team not to oversell. The sales and development teams need to trust that support can keep everyone satisfied by manually walking the last mile if the product yet do so. And the sales and support teams have to trust the development team to get things out when they say they will.

Trust has economic value. It will translate into more sales. Guaranteed.

Sales people rightfully focus on solving pains to make the sale. If there's a pain you've seen arise with several of your customers, the solution goes onto the product roadmap. Is the salesperson 'overselling' when they mention it to new prospects? No.

Will the product team scream they were overselling when the feature isn't released according to the roadmap? 100%.

This isn't meant to pick on the product team. It could just as easily have gone the other way where the sales team is missing their targets.

But everything is that dance.

If the salesperson trusts the product team's estimation and solution, they can confidently say, "You're not the only one facing that issue. In fact, we're addressing it right now and by the time you are fully onboarded, we'll have it ready for you."

Without trust, the response is, "You're not the only one facing that issue. It's on our roadmap and we'll solve it for you (but I won't commit to when)."

Where's the incentive to purchase in the latter case? Why not just wait or find a competitor who already solves it?

Without trust, you have independently functioning silos where work is performed sequentially. That's slow and a guaranteed loser.

Consider These Actions:

- Build empathy. Have everyone share the hardest parts of their job, when they feel like they're letting the team down, and how others can help.

- Job shadow. Once a quarter, randomly pair people up where they each spend a day working with another at their job. Build that 'lost' time into your plans.

- Be transparent and give everyone the space to fail. Commitments need to be hit. If they aren't going to be, it's best everyone knows ahead of time. If that's communicated early enough, others can jump in to assist if the deadline is critical.

- See section: *Hitting Goals, Setting Minimum Metrics*

RESOLVING INTERPERSONAL CHALLENGES

The root of any internal challenge is people. Specifically, how they interact with one another.

Yet nothing is more emotionally draining for you or feels like a greater waste of time than resolving those issues. They aren't strategic, nor do they lead to tangible results.

Except they are and they do.

Performance is highly situational. Put someone in the right role, surrounded by the right people, and they'll succeed. Play them out of position or with a team that operates differently, and they'll suck.

Failing to manage emotions leads to the misuse or underutilization of your employees. Motivation is emotionally driven. Ignoring emotions will drop an employee's performance from being an "A" player to a "B." A "B" to a "C."

Emotional outbursts between workplace colleagues don't just happen. They're the accumulation of many perceived slights built up over time. They are the byproduct of a story that one person has been telling themselves about the other.

We all have these stories about everyone in the building and are all victims of our own confirmation bias. They cause us to color communications with unintended meaning, further exacerbating our issues with our co-workers.

Bridging the humanity gap is your job. In order to keep focus on the goals and what needs to be accomplished, you have to eliminate the other distractions.

Big problems are hard to solve. Small problems, less so. Address issues early and often.

The sooner you write this into your job description, the more you'll be paying attention to interpersonal challenges and the more you'll be able to stifle the stories people tell themselves about one another.

Consider These Actions:

- Game plan with each individual prior to providing solutions. Understand why they are frustrated so they can put their feelings into words. Ask the questions you want them to broach with their teammate:

  - You reacted strongly when Person X suggested [xyz]. Why?

  - How do their actions make you feel?

  - What's a better way they could have gotten the same idea across to you in a way that you'd hear it?

  - How do you think they felt when you reacted?

- Mediate a session. While you will naturally side with one of them, you have to remain neutral so they can hear one another. Reinforce that your role isn't to pick a winner, but to create a space where both feel comfortable contributing their ideas and efforts to the team.

- Double down on the value you see in each, so they feel valued and that they aren't being scapegoated.

- Admit your own failings when they occur. Apologize, explain the feelings you were wrestling with, and ask for advice on how you could have better conveyed your message. You aren't perfect.

HOLDING REMOTE WORKERS TOGETHER

For all our technological advances, human beings still like to talk. And talk. And talk.

There are so many good reasons to work remotely: The solitude to complete work, saving hours of commute time, minimizing office politics, and reinforcing autonomy. Similarly, it's often easier to attract people to hire when you have a national pool rather than just your local area.

But the pendulum has over-swung and we're overlooking the benefits of working together.

Even in the early stages of a company when there are only enough of you to fill the broom closet, it's still a full-time job to keep everyone on the same page.

Every day you're getting new pieces of information that can lead a reasonable person to draw a new conclusion. And that information isn't just coming in through you, but everyone on the team.

Your messages, your priorities, and your focus are drums you need to bang every single day. The more disparate your workforce, the more difficult that becomes.

Equally important, is that as an early-stage company, you do not have all the answers. If you did, you'd be a late-stage company.

It's not just that the answers are unknown, but many of the questions are as well.

What you build, how you sell it, what you charge, how you get customers using it, etc. are all new to you. Even when your product is in the market, there are plenty of improvements to be found.

New solutions are the collision of disparate ideas, often from team members in different groups.

Co-locating allows for happy encounters where teammates from different groups run into one another and hit upon something they may not have come up with individually. It allows for the connecting of dots that many didn't realize were previously relevant.

The argument that everyone gets more done while working remotely is true when the task is known, defined, and discrete. When it's not we require communication and little attention is paid to just how inefficient it is to communicate remotely.

Conversations on group chat platforms not only take significantly longer than when they're conducted in person, but they lack the benefit of body language, inflection, and emotion. There is enormous room for misinterpretation of tone. Misinterpretation creates interpersonal challenges. Resolving those both demand a lot of your time and they are never fully repaired.

Getting your team members to work together and trust one another is difficult enough. Doing it on a high-wire, where the debate of ideas can easily be misinterpreted, makes fostering an atmosphere of improvement—regardless of origin—all the more difficult.

Consider These Actions:
- Always-on video. Bandwidth is plentiful so if people are working remotely, pony up for group video-chat software. Leave it on so even if it's just being able to see people, everyone feels slightly more connected.
- Be the glue. Pay extra attention to the ideas floating around and be the one to connect the dots. People will feel good for being heard and the company will fare better when you introduce the ideas two people had to one another.
- Double the daily standup. Focus on sharing thoughts, concerns and ideas in the daily standup. You need to give space for ideas to bounce around.

MANAGING EMOTIONS, LEADING ACTIVITY

Nobody has a work life and a home life. They just have a life.

There will always be crossover where one affects the other.

Your focus has to be on how to maximize the contribution everyone is making which, like it or not, often requires dealing with things that have nothing to do with the office. The more baggage someone carries, the less effort they are able to apply to their work.

While you can't solve their problems for them, you can hear them out. Providing an outlet and showing that you care is the better part of the battle. Empathy is a far greater tool to create loyalty than money and perks.

Managing emotions often requires checking in when you notice someone is down and giving them the space to feel comfortable sharing what's on their mind. More often than not, it's not what you say, but that you've allowed them to say it, that helps them see things aren't as dire as they appear. That block of time can completely change the individual's, and by extension, the team's effort that week.

Being in the right frame of mind is often more critical than the level of talent on the team. And while you didn't sign up for hearing about others' struggles, you get them whether or not you chose to deal with them. The lost time of listening can unlock a day of effort. That's not a bad return.

Sometimes your job is just to be human.

Consider These Actions:
- Incorporate personal check-ins at your one-on-ones. It's okay to get to know your employees as people. Remember though, you're only their manager in the less important half of their life.
- Get to know something personally meaningful about everyone. Asking about it can open the doors to deeper conversations.
- Keep a scouting report on everyone. Strengths, goals, what triggers negative emotions, external challenges, etc. It helps you stay connected and be an empathetic leader.

CHANNELING EFFORT — MANAGEMENT JUDO

You manage your time, your weight, and your budget. In each, you keep close tabs on changes and take the actions to keep things moving in the line you desire.

Managing implies controlling. It's a verb. You *have* to do something. You believe you aren't doing your job if you're not actively involved.

But there's another way.

Redirecting, not directing.

Every person and every team have energy going down the path they deem best. In order to more efficiently use your time, keep the team performing at its best, and your calendar clear of 'difficult' discussions, consider shifting your mindset.

Rather than forcibly directing a team, redirect the existing energy.

It's management judo.

Baseball managers wear the same uniform as their players. Yet, you can't imagine them on the field, making adjustments to a player's swing during an at-bat or running in front of a player to field a ball.

Instead, coaches take the time to instruct while away from the bright lights so they can tailor their instruction to the player's needs. Coaches take a player's current swing and suggest a slight tweak. They don't (usually) scrap it all and start over.

They're taking advantage of the player's natural abilities and putting them to slightly better use.

It's not being reactive but being efficient. The further you have to bend someone's energy, the more of yours it takes up.

An example of using someone's own energy is taking their interests and applying them to the company's needs. One of our engineers was intrigued by data, yet our product didn't demand computation beyond what was acquired in elementary school. But we had all sorts of data collected on the sales and support side that could make us more efficient at what we did. By better understanding the factors that led to making a sale, a loss, or a churned customer, we could focus our energy far more effectively in a way that led to real financial benefits.

His job was still to write code. He had to help build features, fix bugs, solve problems, etc., but by enabling him to expand his boundary and to pursue his interests, it kept him fired up about doing all those things. He put in extra hours at night working on the data projects because he *wanted* to, not because it was the only time allotted. He was engaged like nobody else because he was able to help other teams and make them better at their jobs.

Not only did he provide visible financial results, but what he learned allowed him to better contribute to product discussions in a way that constructively reshaped the product roadmap. He knew the business better as a result.

Consider These Actions:

- Know your people. Ask them about their professional interests, where they want to be in the next role and the one after that, and what they want to be known for inside your four walls.

- Share the goals and challenges often. Encourage people to explore new ways to reach the goals. Celebrate the effort more than the results.

- Listen. When you feel someone pulling back, ask them what's changed. Only by listening will you know what roadblocks they're facing. Otherwise, your attempts to solve the problem are like a carnival worker trying to guess someone's weight. You may nail it, but often you'll be embarrassingly off.

TAPPING INTRINSIC MOTIVATION

Companies have to make money. Without it, they are simply hobbies.

In the intellectual economy, that means turning your employees' brain waves into real dollars. The more those brain waves emanate, the more opportunity you have to reel in the commas.

To get the most out of your team members, you have to figure out what drives them and give it to them. When you can tap into their own pool of intrinsic motivation, you're creating a competitive advantage on two fronts— inexpensive retention and added effort.

Many companies operate under the assumption that most people are coin operated. You hang a dollar on a fishing pole in front of their face and you can get them to chase it.

The reason is because it's easy and requires no customization. It's lazy.

Motivating extrinsically doesn't require managers to have any managing skill whatsoever. It creates a transactional relationship that feeds off increasingly expensive inputs. I give you a dollar in exchange for output. With time, that dollar is assumed and motivates less. Another dollar is required to get the same output for which you'd previously only paid a buck.

Extrinsic motivators are easily matched by every other company out there. But other companies are rarely able to match an interest in the *person* attached to the pair of hands typing on the keyboard. Feeding intrinsic motivations doesn't provide a diminishing return.

But you can't just assume you know what drives someone else. You have to ask.

Why does an employee work (once a minimum salary threshold is met)? When they do great work, how do they want to be rewarded? What do they want to learn? When they close their eyes, in what role do they imagine themselves?

It's not as easy as just asking those questions, however. Getting real, honest, insightful answers is difficult for two reasons. One, most people haven't been asked before, so they've rarely given it much thought. And two, it requires the employee trust you with something intimate—something they may not have even admitted to themselves before.

To earn their trust, you must first give it.

Show your own vulnerability and entrust them with it. Eventually, they will do the same.

Trust is a repeated process.

When you're trusted to handle your employee's professional arc with care, you've created something that your competitors are unlikely to achieve.

It often requires putting your teammates and company's needs ahead of your own, which is why it's a brutally effective competitive advantage. Few others are willing to do so.

Consider These Actions:

- Assign homework. It's more than just asking people what they need because few will have given it much thought. They absolutely know when they *aren't* getting it, but they can rarely point you in the right direction. Put it on them to figure it out.

- Share your needs. When you can open up about the things you need and show that ego is just a thing we all have, you will give them permission to explore their own.

- Start small. If searching for someone's internal motivation isn't something you already practice, start with just an employee or two. (Give yourself the chance to succeed and start with the most open, engaged employees.)

- Provide constant feedback. Focus on what's going well and give them the kudos they deserve. If there are shortcomings, ask for suggestions on how you can help reach the next level.

LEADING WITH QUESTIONS

Even if you're confident enough in your abilities to admit you don't have all the answers, getting the information required to have a few more is enormously difficult.

Most founders have started a company because they are fairly adept at processing disparate information and assembling it into something of value. You wouldn't have seen a solution in the market where others didn't if that weren't the case.

But without information, your value stagnates.

You are in the information business. Customers, employees, vendors, investors, journalists— everyone has something that you need to know. Everyone has a piece of information which, on its own, may be meaningless, but when combined with another's piece, may be the key that unlocks a door you've been trying to break down.

But nobody is going to volunteer the most useful information—not because they don't want to but, because it's not top of mind, they aren't aware of its existence or they assume everyone knows it.

Similarly, you don't always know what information of value they possess.

Play dumb. It is the most effective way to listen and to get people to talk more.

It's also one of the most effective ways to encourage action. When questions lead employees to the right answers, they see the path and rationale far more clearly than if you'd prescribed the path. And, who knows, you may find something in the process that unlocks something new for you.

Putting your ego aside is one of the hardest things to do. Yes, it's your company, but you have to trust that, by relinquishing your 'authority,' you will get more effort and value in the long term. It's an investment.

Consider These Actions:
- Seek out rationale, not opinions. Often, people aren't totally sure why they think what they think. Keep asking why. Don't stop until you're satisfied with the rationale. The Japanese ask '5 whys' to get to the heart of a problem. Do likewise.

- Be a bad lawyer. Ask leading questions when you feel the need to shift opinions. Ask how likely they think [xyz] bad outcome is to happen, why it might happen, and how they'd mitigate it. If they don't have good responses, it gets them thinking more deeply about the challenge or, better, open to alternative approaches.
- Seek feedback on your solution. Not only does it provide more alternatives to avoid the traps, but by providing a solution, it creates space for others to accept the idea as their own since their 'yeah buts' get rationally addressed.

MEETING GOALS BY WORKING BACKWARD

Do-or-die goals, like acquiring new investors, are tricky beasts that use misdirection to allude entrepreneurs. Whether it's raising money or hitting financial targets, you have a major milestone you've identified that probably hasn't been broken down enough to engender any confidence in meeting it.

Major milestones are typically not met alone. They are the product of having met numerous other goals.

Working backward from your desired end-state helps to open your thinking as to what needs to happen to get there, what dead-ends you'll face along the way, what risks come with success, etc.

In other words, working backward helps you plan.

The exercise gets you thinking about what happens when one goal is met. For example, when sales lands those five large accounts, who will onboard all five in the same week? What processes need automation to onboard them all with a single employee?

The odds of achieving monetary success are long. You're fighting for every percentage point, trying to tip them in your favor. Few are bigger than anticipating the challenges your own success will throw at you. If you can work backward to solve for small success, you will often find big success.

Consider These Actions:
- Five whats. A riff on the Japanese process of getting to the heart of a problem by asking '5 Whys', the Five Whats help you identify the pre-requisites for each stage. If you need to raise funding, what needs to happen prior? If the goal is to achieve $XX,000 in MRR, what do you need to do to achieve your MRR goal? Retain 90% of customers? What do you need to retain those customers? Etc.
- Focus on the fundamentals of revenue. While the next step need not always be revenue-based, you must know the drivers of your business to raise capital. For example, keeping customers is just as important, and cheaper, than acquiring new ones.
- Look beyond the product. Your product is a means to making money, not the goal in itself. If goals are product-centric, have a strong point of view

(model it out) of how it will lead to new customers, keep old ones, or generate new revenue.

HITTING GOALS, SETTING MINIMUM METRICS

Setting goals is the obvious and universally recommended approach to generate progress, but how they get set is too often self-defeating.

We unknowingly self-sabotage ourselves via the metrics we set. Bars set too high can't be cleared. And when we fail to clear them, they reinforce our self-doubts and create a deflating pattern for teams.

Every time we set a goal and miss, we reduce the urgency to hit the next one.

Stretch goals are easily excused; they weren't intended to be hit. Minimum metrics are not. Few good excuses exist for missing what you should hit 90% of the time.

With those success rates, it becomes meaningful and very painful when they're missed. It forces self-reflection because it's rare. Hitting them may not change the immediate trajectory of the company, but it creates a cycle of consistency that gets others to believe. It creates accountability because the expectation is that everyone clears their bar. It builds the muscle of progress.

If you find the company missing targets, it's likely because the targets were crafted more from the need to reach the next milestone, rather than an understanding of what it takes to get there. Failure to hit targets is a condemnation of the process to set them more so than the process to reach them. The team pays for it, but that's on you.

You want your goals to focus effort and to provide a feedback loop. Feedback loops are fuel. Everyone wants to know the score and how they're performing. Putting points on the board (i.e. reaching goals) begets a desire to put up more. It builds a belief that everyone and every team can take on the Goliath in the industry.

If your goals underscore your team's failures, then you're better off not having goals at all.

Setting realistic goals isn't easy. Following through on them is even harder.

Things come up that you weren't anticipating, and it'll be easy to excuse the fact that you missed the goals.

But something *always* comes up to shift the priorities. Always. Plan for it now by setting the minimum bar.

Consider These Actions:

- Design goals from the bottom up to root them in reality. For example, how many phone calls and e-mails can a salesperson make in a month? What's the rate of demos? How many produce a proposal? What percent close? If you know how active you want sales and/or business-development reps to be at the front end, realistic sales goals can follow.

- Set goals you'll hit 90% of the time. Just like needing to provide a handful of positive comments for every 'constructive' one, your goal for goals should be to get everyone in the habit of hitting them (the positive), so that when you need to ask everyone to dig in (the constructive) they are willing to do so.

- Revisit monthly goals every week. You can course correct after a week but can't when there's only a week to go.

- Be comfortable readjusting. As you learn more, you'll realize some of the goals you set weren't the top priorities to begin with.

- Be transparent about progress so everyone can ask for help. If you're halfway through the month and a quarter of the way through reaching a goal, it's time to call in the cavalry. Start this yourself to remove the stigma associated with admitting you won't meet what you thought you could.

AVOIDING INTERNAL COMPETITIONS

Competitions are page one of the lazy leader's playbook.

Competitions create improvement. That's true in marketplaces and (often) for individuals. But your company is a team. Teams have to work together in order to succeed.

Your job is to motivate everyone to accomplish the things most others see as too hard to try. Most competitions promote individual achievement over the team. Why would you willingly do something where only one employee (the winner) feels good about their efforts?

If your goal is to motivate, you succeed with one while failing with n-1.

Internal competitions focus energy and attention, but not always on the things that matter most. Rather than being laser focused on the prospects, customers, and competitors—all of whom live outside your four walls—there is an eye kept on the teammates involved in the competition.

They may drive better results in the near-term. But people can only sprint for so long and others can only lose so many times before both groups run out of gas.

You have the perfect competition right in front of you. It exists in the marketplace; you don't need to artificially create a new one internally.

If there isn't enough competition in the marketplace to fuel everyone's competitive juices and push them to improve, then either your market is too small, or your team doesn't know enough about the market to care. Going toe-to-toe with bigger, better capitalized foes should fire up everyone keen on working for an early-stage company to find cheaper, faster, smarter solutions.

Consider These Actions:
- Compete against your past performance. Most who run marathons don't have a goal of winning, but of besting their personal record. Motivation and improvement are possible without naming losers.
- Set team-wide goals. Everyone knows how much they contribute toward the goal and will want to step it up on their own. Crafting competitions around team efforts will encourage everyone to help others to their feet

should they trip. It will push everyone to share something they've found to work better than the old way. It will encourage more communication because their interconnectedness is highlighted by the results.

- Craft macro-competitions around the biggest challenges you have. For example, if you need the product team to be more responsive to existing customers rather than on new features, create a company-wide competition around reducing churn.

STOKING EFFORT WITH ATTENTION

Your attention is how you demonstrate respect. When you make it difficult for employees to catch your attention, you're telling them where they stand in your list of priorities. Treat them like your customer.

There are so many channels we have to monitor these days: e-mail, group chat, text, phone, drop-ins, etc. It's overwhelming and you'd be excused for not being able to monitor them all.

But you have to be great at responding to <u>one</u> of them.

Set the expectation that you will get back to people 100% of the time within a certain period of time through at least that single channel.

You know how much you hate having to remember to follow up on requests you've made to employees? That feeling is mutual.

When you are unresponsive, you're preventing your employees from doing their job. You are choosing to prioritize your efforts over theirs. You are choosing to make the employee both slower and worse at their job.

Pick a channel and a deadline. You'll respond by the end of the day to e-mails or perhaps within four or five hours on chat or two days by phone. If you hate using one, don't use it. But make sure everyone knows that.

It's your job to set the expectation for the channel, response time, level of request that should be surfaced to you, and what to do if it's more urgent.

Your employees are your customers. You would never ignore a customer, so why would you ever do so with your employees?

Consider These Actions:
- Eliminate one channel immediately. For example, voicemail doesn't work for me. So, I allowed my voicemail box to fill up and haven't emptied it in years. If you know me, you know how to reach me.
- Just listen. Often, people aren't looking for an answer but are seeking your approval for the path they're traversing to get to an answer. Single sentence responses are often good enough. But, if you can't tell what they're seeking, you must ask.

- Hold office hours. Office hours block out the time for you so you're not beating yourself up for not completing something, and it allows you to devote your full attention to those who need you.

CREATING FOCUS BY SLOWING DOWN

When you dance with elephants, you're quick or you're dead.

It's one of my favorite descriptions of the mentality needed to thrive as a small, early-stage company. But speed isn't a byproduct of working faster.

Speed is a function of focus and the motivation to execute.

And while you are constantly thinking of new ways to spur sales or the next feature that changes the game, creating focus and motivation is the real job.

Unfortunately, ideas are speed's kryptonite. Though they may be what the business needs they (usually) help neither focus nor motivation.

It's your company; everyone naturally looks to you for directional clues. People want to be invaluable and will do their best to align their focus with the direction the company's headed. All of which work well until you cloud the direction with 'updated' thinking, riffed thoughts, or the request for feedback on new ideas.

The line between founder-teammate collaboration and founder directive is wide and blurry. You will be shocked when some take a half-baked idea you're just testing out and assume it to be the new priority.

The result is your team starts pulling, ever so slightly, in different directions. Someone will see the reason your idea will work and start pulling in that direction, while others are still convinced the last idea was the best one and be pulling tangentially.

Meanwhile, you've gone back to your desk to think about the next idea, assuming everyone knew that you were just spit balling and looking for feedback.

While the directions they're pulling are all in the same hemisphere, you need them to be in the same narrow vector to be successful.

The wider that vector the more chaotic things feel. Chaos is negatively correlated to the trust others have in you and it slows what seems like an already glacial execution timeline.

No matter what your velocity or how impressive the product quality, the company and the product will *never* reach what you envision when you close your eyes. It can be disheartening and will cause some entrepreneurs to push harder and place blame at the team's feet for the pace of play.

The real challenge is to slow things down. The caveat is that you must slow things down *in your own head*. You will always be able to think and learn faster than any team will execute. Slowing things down in your head means giving your teams the space to complete the last identified priority before banging the drum on the next. It will feel maddeningly slow, but when you look back a year later, the accomplishments will be more significant than if you'd 'failed fast.'

Consider These Actions:

- Find someone to challenge your ideas. If you have someone in your circle who can tell you when the emperor has no clothes, recruit them to regularly sit with you (frequency depends on your ability to avoid shiny objects) to challenge the assumptions behind your ideas and give you the reason to say, "no."

- Write down the priorities and philosophies and repeat often. Why you're doing what you're doing, what needs to happen, how you improve, etc. Evaluate ideas against each of them.

- Keep track of your 'new ideas.' If you give them a home (a notebook reserved just for the ideas or in a sticky note app on your phone), then you won't feel as strong a need to publicize them internally. The more you can keep them to yourself, the more your team can focus. Only if you keep coming back to it each week is it *potentially* worth discussing more broadly.

- Only pursue multiplier ideas. If it doesn't make things several times faster or more profitable, shelve it. You need game-changing improvements early. Single-digit improvements are for publicly traded companies.

GIVING PERFORMANCE REVIEWS

When you feel like there's no time to do the internal work you only make life harder for yourself in the future.

Everyone needs a feedback loop. We are all motivated by recognition in one form or another and want to be known for having done great work.

But the historical system to provide that feedback—the annual performance review —runs counter to everything it hopes to achieve: improvement, engagement, and understanding. It's a mess.

The annual review is not a course correction but more like a Roman emperor giving a thumbs up or down to promotions, raises, and new assignments. It's evaluative, not instructive.

If you believe your team can and should get better every day, then you need a more involved approach.

Imagine learning to play the drums. After a year of practicing, your instructor sits with you to tell you all the things you'd done doing wrong. He'll raise an example of a specific song that you played ten months ago to illustrate the point.

You don't recall that or believe the feedback sounds like something you'd have done. Either way, you reject it and, likely, harbor a bit of animosity toward the instructor.

A feedback loop is most impactful as soon after a teachable moment as possible.

The reasons to give feedback quickly are manifold, including:
- It gives you the chance to continually reiterate the positive. In youth sports, the 5:1 ratio of positive comments to constructive comments is a gold standard. We adults may have the armor to deal with a reduced ratio, but that doesn't mean we don't still need to positive. When feedback is given quickly, there aren't a lot of negatives available to pile up that would require a truckload of positives to counterbalance.
- There is no recency bias distorting your feedback.
- It's less personal. The quick feedback is focused on a specific example and you can be instructive about the moment rather than setting up the

criticism as a personal trait. For example, try "When we were talking about the roadmap, you pushed back really hard on the timing but didn't give any rationale for why it wasn't possible. Can you share those reasons with me now?" instead of months later, "You often default to timing never being possible instead of helping the team find ways to get it done." The former is descriptive of the moment, the latter is declarative about their personality.

- Everything is top of mind. You can ask what they need you to do to help and they will likely have some ideas instead of the employee spending months assuming you're not willing to do anything to fix what's broken.

Consider These Actions:

- Use one-on-ones as the feedback cycle. This is the time to parse out small bits of constructive feedback without turning anyone too far sideways. Small issues are easier to address than large ones.

- Build a feedback loop to the feedback loop. If your feedback creates the desired change, but that change goes unrecognized then it may as well have not happened in the first place. Everyone needs acknowledgement of the effort it took to do things differently.

- Make it bilateral. You should be seeking feedback in each of your one-on-ones as well. When you're open to it, hear it, and attempt to improve, your team members will be far more likely to do likewise.

- Have fun with it. This is your opportunity to help them in their career. You get to highlight their efforts and ensure they are getting what they want professionally.

- Solve for the disease, not the symptom. This means leading with questions to get the point across without creating an issue. "I've noticed you seemed distracted and you're not producing the same quantity/quality of work the last couple of weeks. Is there anything causing this? What can I do to help you get back to your usual level?"

GIVING FEEDBACK IN THE ONE-ON-ONE

"Come on, we can make it quick."

Too frequently that's the prelude to the one-on-one.

You don't just put your product into the marketplace and not expect feedback that will help you improve. Yet we do this every week with our people. Everyone needs feedback.

One-on-one meetings with your team members are one of the most important things you can do this week. It's your chance to learn about the challenges the teams face, the interpersonal dynamics that could undermine your goals, and the things you've said that have been misconstrued. It's also your opportunity to give feedback on areas of individual improvement.

Every one-on-one is a chance to shore up the foundation of your company and improve upon it.

Never cancel them.

Never minimize their importance.

Never walk into one totally unprepared.

These blocks of time—done right—can be a safe zone where the employee can get their concerns out and where you can provide bite-sized performance evaluations.

Consistent connection builds trust. That trust is critical. The more trust others have in you and how you'll react to what they tell you, the more they'll share.

Trust is only earned through your actions and time. Having a solid block to reconnect with someone is your chance to advance that trust by following through on the prior items to which you've committed, showing empathy, listening, and showing you can protect their concerns from the team.

Trust is the result of a repeated game. One-on-ones are that game.

One-on-ones feel like a management task that must be done, but one that doesn't move the needle. You are going to see the meeting notification pop up and dread it. It won't feel important because half a dozen times in a row, nothing of great import was shared between the two of you. You'll be left thinking about all the other things you could accomplish during this time.

Punting these meetings leads to the long and unproductive white board sessions in a soulless, off-site conference room. Putting off the one-on-one has a compounding effect that leads to unproductive.

While this meeting belongs to the employee, it's to your benefit.

Consider These Actions:

- Set the expectations about preparation to ensure the employee gets their questions answered, concerns heard, and professional goals met.
- Lead with questions. People will often hint at what's happening, but not dig into specifics. Use questions to help focus on the heart of the issue and to get the employee to think about solving it themselves.

    - Why would you have handled that differently?
    - How would you prefer that decision have been made?
    - Remain silent. Nobody is comfortable with silence and will usually reveal more.

- Review the discussion from the prior meeting. You want your employee to know you heard them and that you're keeping their thoughts in mind. If there were actions on either side, you need to hold you both accountable.
- Be prepared. Have a couple of items or examples you want to discuss ready. You don't have to spend more than five or ten minutes prior to the meeting, but the preparation will show you value the employee.

MEASURING NON-FINANCIAL SUCCESS

You've likely spent a lot of time envisioning what the future looks like when your product is good…and ubiquitous. You have an intuition of what success feels like when everyone is using your product.

You've set the bar for success as perfection and, unwittingly, opened yourself up for failure by not crediting yourself with anything short of that.

But most things are out of your control. The timing of the market, passage of new legislation, the macro-economy, etc.

It's important to focus on the things you can control in order to validate your success. And to keep you focused on what matters.

While the people who do the work are at the heart of everything we do, we rarely measure our impact in there. The human side is fuzzy and hard to control so we don't take the time to measure it.

The reality, however, is that it is the one area you have the most control. Who you allow to walk through your doors is at your discretion and expending the effort to bring out the best in others is a decision that's yours to make.

The people on the team are the ones who score the points. Adding their desire to chase success to your personal metrics is the best way to increase your odds of finding financial success.

In the end, all anyone can control is effort. Ideally, the outcome takes care of itself, but measuring outcomes alone breeds a lot of false results that can cause you anguish and increase doubt.

Hiring
We rarely credit ourselves with making a good hire or even making a 'fine' hire that isn't destructive. Assembling a team is difficult and doing it in a way that doesn't blow everything up deserves recognition.

Engagement
The effort people are willing to give each day is a reflection of your ability to engage them. When people go above and beyond to cross the finish line, you should privately take a little slice of credit for creating an environment in which they could flourish.

Accountability

When you hear someone take ownership of a poor result, let yourself smile. That's not possible if you've created a retributive environment where employees feel pitted against one another.

Everything people-oriented is difficult to measure, but the absence of complete dysfunction in the uncertain face of changing a market is, in itself, success.

Consider These Actions:

- Create the process to integrate new hires into your system. The process to add to your team is more important than the process to onboard customers, and yet we give it a fraction of the thought.

- Track engagement regularly. Send out a survey *at least* monthly to help understand how much people believe in the game plan and their level of confidence in their team, in you, and the long-term prospects of the company. It's not the number today that matters, but the trend line for each individual. Engagement is fickle and can flip in a single conversation. Today's rating has little correlation to tomorrow's.

- Give everyone the power to police. Managing culture is not a one-person job. Everyone has to own it. Beyond just giving everyone the expectations by which they should interact, you must provide the tools to police.

    - How do you approach someone who misstepped and didn't live up to the cultural expectations? When do you do it? How do you make it impersonal?

MISTAKING 'F' PLAYERS FOR 'A' PLAYERS

What should you do with an employee you know is a problem but delivers results? Sometimes 'F' players hide beneath 'A' clothing.

It is easy to be blinded by wins and focus on the one who crosses the finish line. Positive results paper over the path it took to get there, no matter how destructive.

Some of the most dangerous employees you have will be the ones who succeed brilliantly without regard for how it affects others on the team.

The star gets your recognition and is rewarded.

Blindly rewarding the outcome sends a signal that getting the job done by any means necessary is expected. People trump teams.

The resulting outcome-based reward system can be devastating if and when people shut down, depart, or ruthlessly compete against one another.

How we interact with one another matters. Not because we're nice, but because we're human. Most people have no desire to put forth effort after feeling unappreciated, harassed, or dismissed.

This was highlighted in spades when I was working at a trendy, high-flying startup. I'm not being coy to hide the identities of innocent, but I couldn't even begin to tell you what we did to describe it further. We were an idea with a ton of funding, chasing a better idea that actually solved a problem that could someday make money.

The one thing this company did better than most was hire. We had outstanding people. Of the 30 non-executives, six started new companies (including some with big exits) and several others are now senior executives with companies doing tens of millions in revenue.

One employee, in particular, was doing a fantastic job. By all traditional measures, he was the most productive amongst us. He was the star.

But he was also in it for himself. He was mistrusting and couldn't hear solutions that weren't his own. Over time, everyone shut down. Why bother offering to contribute if the executive team was going to default to him and he was blind to alternative approaches? Everyone in his orbit got worse.

When you tally up his contribution and net out the loss from everyone else, he was an unobjective net negative. He was an 'F' player in 'A' clothing.

Business is a team sport. Sometimes individuals carry the team, but often only because others did the unflashy work. Reward accordingly.

Consider These Actions:

- Be intentional about *what* you reward. If you seek teamwork, you should recognize those who pitched in at the expense of their "real" jobs. If you seek a workplace where you want everyone to stay in their lanes and hustle, then you will want to focus on the extraordinary effort that went into the result.

- Roll interpersonal dynamics into your one-on-ones. Asking everyone who has been the most helpful to the team each week will help you determine who has the respect of others and help you keep the focus on the right behaviors.

- Don't hire the pseudo A-players in the first place. Make the interviewee show you that they have worked in the manner you're seeking in the past. They won't conform to your wishes or the cultural norms just because you hired them. Past behaviors are always an indicator of future actions.

MISTAKING 'A' PLAYERS FOR 'C' PLAYERS

Not everyone looks like an 'A' player. Optimizing team performance requires social performances that tend to go unrecognized. The burden is borne by the social Sherpa who helps everyone reach their respective peaks.

Each time you add a new hire, you introduce a new variable to the team's dynamic. That additional node in the communication flow affects every existing team member.

No matter how much effort you apply toward making teams function well, there are some things you just can't tackle. Someone within the group has to authentically assume those responsibilities. These are the things that typically go unrecognized but that bind a team together. They include:

- translating differing ideas so others can consider them;
- authentically coordinating time to get to know one another;
- befriending other functions;
- bridging communication needs;
- connecting people in different groups with symbiotic ideas;
- providing energy when others are lacking; and
- holding others accountable to their short-term, daily commitments.

There are so many things that are required to maintain and nurture a team's health. Very few are written into a job description. But every functional team has someone selflessly tending to those gaps at the expense of their 'real' job.

Their willingness to carry that load shouldn't diminish your evaluation of their formalized effort. In the end, replacing the skills to do the 'real' role is stupidly simple. Replacing the glue that endears camaraderie, trust, and communication, less so.

For example, one of my first interactions with a colleague after I entered the once Byzantine Empire of Yahoo:

> Me, mumbling at my inbox: "Mmph. Are you %#^&ing kidding?"
> Co-worker, looking to be helpful: "Who's blocking you?"
> Me: "The Front-Page team."
> Co-worker: "We need to talk to Katie. She makes everything run."

<moments later>
Co-worker: "Okay we have coffee with her in 20 minutes. I'll introduce you guys and we'll get it squared away."

Yahoo had five-figure headcount when I joined, half of whom were in newly specialized roles that had been created that same calendar year. Teams were suddenly twice as large, so the same work had twice as many hurdles to clear. It was a mess.

I'd been hired in for a specialized role that was about one shoebox wide in scope. A simple job that required maximizing the flow of traffic on the Yahoo network to one particular property. There were others doing the same for other properties and the role required horse trading with every other group in the company in order to succeed.

The only reason these roles were even remotely successful was because of one guy. He was my peer who held the same job. He was good, but not a star by traditional outcome-based measures.

Yet, he was one of the most important players within Yahoo as far as optimizing revenue generation. None of us would have been remotely effective without him.

He knew *everyone*.

He was seemingly one-degree away from the person you needed to know in order to get any job done. He made every single person around him better.

Yet, he was never promoted and eventually let go in one of the numerous downsizing efforts. Nobody recognized the value he created because the measured output of his job wasn't breaking any records. But he was responsible for optimizing hundreds of millions in actual revenue during his tenure.

Nobody saw it. He was an 'A' player hiding in 'C' clothing.

Consider These Actions:

- Incorporate social context into performance. People aren't just in control of their effort and output, but in their attitudes and interactions with everyone around them.
- In your one-on-ones, always ask who is doing great work. You'll get answers that are less outcome-based and more around who is being most helpful to the team.

- Track the invisible. "Engagement" is over-used and sloppily defined but gather consistent data on people's desire to give effort. Track regularly and frequently so you have context and can solve problems before they get too big to solve.

- Be Socratic. Ask teams if they understand what priorities other groups have, why those are the way they are, and what challenges they face. If the team understands and can speak to the rationale of others, it means someone is doing a great job of communicating internally.

MANAGING SALARY EXPENSES

There will come a time when employee costs will seem out of control. But there is a difference between being frugal and being cheap. Frugality keeps the doors open, cheapness caps upside.

Not all expenses are costs. There is one line on the bottom half of the income statement that's guaranteed to generate a return.

Payroll.

Maximizing your return on every employee is almost as critical as never running out of money.

Doing so is often squishy, time-consuming, and not fun.

Salary should not be the primary selling point for working for you. But it shouldn't be a pain point either. Everyone needs to be paid enough to not have to worry about living. That's easier said than done in the early days when you need to cut corners on every expense.

But sometimes that extra couple thousand dollars you save is the difference between feeling valued and wanting to look around. It's often an unspoken test, and one that is awfully expensive, in terms of your time, a team's opportunity cost, and the reinvestment into new hires, should you fail.

As revenue comes in, the natural tendency is to reinvest in new hires or new channels. The thinking assumes that the existing workforce is a given; that you'll get what you get and that they aren't going anywhere. But sometimes the best investment is into the one you already have. This is particularly true if you had to cut corners on all those early employees. Reinvesting in your employees can be good business.

When I first arrived to run Distillery Solutions, it's not a stretch to say that everyone was paid 50-80% of what they'd have made elsewhere. As a bootstrapped company, that was what the budget allowed. My goal was to ratchet everyone up to market without putting the company in financial danger.

I was constantly on the lookout for ways to shave expenses by 2%. Sometimes I found more, other times less. But over almost three years, the non-payroll operating expense had been cut by a third despite our top line growing three times. Most of those dollars were reinvested back into wages. We cut fat and turned it into muscle (recognition leads to effort); more output for the same cost.

Investing in people, both new and existing, is where you find your return, not due to a soft, altruistic approach but simply because it was critical to recognize that success was a team effort.

For most companies operating in the knowledge economy, your people are ultimately your product.

Your customers are buying your people. It's your people, after all, that are creatively solving problems via a delivered product.

Money isn't your strongest lever to motivate, but it is one of the strongest levers to *demotivate*. If people are worried about covering rent or feel they are being treated unfairly in comparison to their teammates, then motivation becomes difficult to muster.

The real expense is slowing or shedding revenue.

Consider These Actions:

- Cut 2% of non-payroll expenses every quarter. You may get there, you may not. But for every few hundred dollars a month you save, you're that much closer to investing in more help or making someone feel incredibly valued.

- Don't pay for SaaS contracts upfront until you've used them for at least six-months. Make your team prove there is value in it beforehand.

- Pair reinvestment opportunities to revenue goals. For example, it can cost as little as a few hundred dollars per employee per month to establish a 401k (without a match). Set a revenue target to pay for it around which everyone can rally.

PRODUCT

In the advertising world it's said that half of your ad budget is wasted, but nobody knows which half.

The same can be said for product development efforts. Half the debate over priorities, half the scaffolding built to facilitate scale, and half the features are wasted.

The sections that follow don't prescribe how to build products. But rather, how to gain a little bit of that wasted time back by cutting off the oxygen to the noisy opinion bubbles.

Building a product is a creative endeavor. And as with most creative pursuits everyone has an opinion, regardless of taste or knowledge.

Ultimately, every challenge has a dozen solutions, ten of which will work.

Unless you're graced with clairvoyance or a refusal to learn, picking the one that will work best years in the future is likely a matter of preference.

Imagine you were designing a house. Your preference may be to build one with the master bedroom on the top floor so it is more appealing when the time comes to sell while I prefer one with a bedroom on the main floor so I can age in place. You may prefer brick while I prefer stone.

We each have the goal of crafting something that will provide a warm, dry place to spend our nights. Both approaches will work. Both can be 'right.'

It's a matter of preference.

Preference debates burn time.

And while today's product approaches tell you to let your customers determine what gets built, it's not always possible with B2B products. B2B products are fundamentally different than consumer products.

Buying committees ensure that's the case.

Gathering information from the end users may result in an amazing solution, but they don't have the checkbook. Collecting priorities from the buyer may leave end users grousing about the product's inability to solve the core challenge. Best case, you thread the needle and build just enough to sell it and to provide value. More realistically, you have a Franken-product that partially solves every group's problems but addresses none of them well enough to replace the status quo.

Hours turn to weeks and weeks become months as you debate what's really *minimum* in MVP. You'll still get there, but it will take longer.

The priorities of competing constituencies burn time.

Further complicating matters is that most (likely including you) aren't knowledgeable enough about the market to know what you don't know. Everyone is learning the customer needs as you build.

And when you know relatively little that next chunk of information can dramatically change your point of view. Those new chunks create a priority whipsaw.

Whipsaws burn time.

None of this is to say you shouldn't learn, shouldn't listen to your customers, or shouldn't lean on your team's knowledge. This isn't mutually exclusive to having an open, collaborative environment but it requires creating a mindset that allows everyone to focus. It creates a tight sieve through which all ideas are run and only the game changers come out the bottom.

As the founder, even if you don't write code, you're building the sieve that buys focus. The mindset that buys time. (Or rather, that wastes less of it.)

You will still always feel like you're one idea away from winning that next customer, changing the marketplace entirely, or attracting an investor's check, but it's a mirage.

The idea is worthless until it's executed.

And it is years of steady execution that is the bedrock to overnight success. That execution occurs during the quiet time that is free of the incessant barrage of 'better' ideas.

Say "no," focus, repeat.

FINDING PRODUCT-GUT FIT

The path to finding product-market fit is a wonderful concept: Knock the smallest thing possible together to find out whether people will pay. Only then should you spend massive amounts of time and money to build it.

But it should not be a universal, unquestioned approach. For one, it's often only blindingly obvious in hindsight.

Another is that the B2B enterprise world has differences that make the approach more confounding.

Quite often, people don't know what they want. The quip of what would have happened if Henry Ford asked people what they want has some truth to it. They'd have asked for faster horses, not cars.

Worse, they know what they want but don't have the budget (i.e. they want a pony but can only afford a guinea pig).

Further, an enterprise's group decision-making process isn't terribly conducive to customer-driven roadmaps. Group product design leads to jack-a-lopes, not unicorns.

This principle isn't solely applicable to the select few who are creating new industries. Reapplying existing ideas in new ways—which is arguably just about everything—will require some level of education in order to sell. The more you must educate *en masse*, the less useful the idea of quickly testing product-market fit becomes.

When you know that the approach in your gut is the right one, act upon it.

Consider These Actions:
- Focus on the problems and the *reasons* they exist. People are usually better at improving upon something that already exists as opposed to identifying the piece that isn't there. Get them to focus on what they know while you intuit what they don't.
- Shadow your customers. Understand where the product fits within their day so you can focus on not just functionality but on making it easier to incorporate into their lives.

- Create a customer roundtable who have proven insightful and present them with storyboards. Ask them to help balance the trade-off between functionality and time.

PRIORITIZING FOR POWER CENTERS

You may be thinking: If the end user sees the value, they'll convince others to buy. But there's a power structure for which you have to account.

Every company has a power center. It's the group that basically gets blank checks and can dictate terms to other internal groups.

Selling into the enterprise is often an exercise in political science. There's a group of people who you must convince. Some can write a check, others will use your product, and others will claim expertise in your field. Everyone can say 'no.' Few can say 'yes.'

Except for those within a power center. They can log an overriding 'yes' vote if you convince them your product is required.

Can you tailor your product to address those power centers? If not, can you augment your product with a services team to become invaluable to that group?

For example, in many companies, sales is a power center. Revenue is how the company is evaluated so the sales engine almost always gets what it believes it needs to be successful. That's power.

You can use these power dynamics to your advantage to force the issue with the power center to get your product in the door. A test inside the power center is more valuable than five tests elsewhere. If you become critical within the power center, you are sticking around for a long time.

It's not always sales. It could be engineering, finance, or corporate development. Find the power center and you'll increase win rates and decrease churn.

Consider These Actions:
- Find the rewards. Knowing how any buyer is rewarded is critical but playing within the reward zone of the power center is the center of the Tootsie Pop™. Can your product contribute to the work that's rewarded?
- Adjust a few degrees. It's not necessarily about changing your product as it is changing how that value is presented. It needs to be viewed from the perspective of the buyer and not exclusively the end user. Providing value

to the power center sometimes creates more work for the end user. So be it. A powerful advocate can override an annoyed user.

- Add those in power centers to your customer roundtable, especially if they aren't the end user. Their insights may not always top the priority list, but they can be useful to the sales and account management teams to help the actual users show the value you create. And the product ideas they muster can help you become critical to a constituency that ensure you win the renewal.

BUILDING FOR THE LAZY

People don't need your product. More to the point, they don't know they do.

There are so many products that would be amazing if founders could just get people to use them. But that's a big ask when the benefits are not entirely and immediately clear.

Everyone has enough apps in their life, enough tasks to do, and enough appointments for which they're already late. Squeezing one more item onto the task list isn't helpful. You will never convince anyone you're actually saving them time.

You need to show value immediately and repeatedly. If you can do so from the first click without requiring anything from the user, you'll be more likely to get something from them in return.

Solve for lazy to succeed.

An experienced founder with whom I worked created a sales coaching app. It was an amazing product. They'd broken down the enterprise sales process to various components that, when applied within the process, would translate to real results (i.e. revenue).

Collecting evaluative data for each sales representative showed them exactly what they needed to do to sell more. Over time, the sales rep would see their performance improve (i.e. increased close rates and compensation).

Meanwhile, the sales manager would look like a star, because her team was producing better than ever.

All that was missing was the evaluative data. The challenge was that the customer's sales reps couldn't evaluate themselves and, often, when the customer's sales manager went on ride-alongs with the rep, they wound up taking over the conversation and doing the selling themselves.

This company literally sold revenue, yet sales were sluggish. Until they solved for lazy.

Instead of banking on changing people's behavior, they did it for them. Outsourcing the evaluative assessments offshore to teachers (an audience familiar with grading others) they were able to seed the app with enough information to pique the interest of rep and manager alike to get them to put more and better data in themselves.

Performing the heavy lift for their customers got the flywheel started enough to prove that taking action was going to be worth the end users' time.

Consider These Actions:

- Design into users' lives rather than simply designing the product experience. What are they *already* doing in their day on which you can piggyback?
- Do it for them. When you're reliant upon people doing things they've never done and have little incentive to do, you need to show them the value in order to prove it's worth their time.
- Find immediate value. With nothing but a click or two, is it possible to demonstrate the value extracted with more involvement? Show it right off the bat.

SAYING NO AND SOLVING ONE PROBLEM

One of the biggest differences between an established, traditional company and a startup is often, counterintuitively, the breadth of their solution.

The startup that is 'an end-to-end solution' or has a description rife with commas is likely to fail. The reason is a lack of focus. The traditional competitors have, over time, homed in on one particular problem and attacked it relentlessly. It's a problem on which they've been able to generate a lot of revenue. It's a winning formula.

Yet, for many of us, we try to out-compete them by offering more despite employing far fewer. It's not rational.

Our ability to say, "no" allows us to more precisely define who we are, what we do, and why we're in business. Focus can sell.

One of the first weeks in an accelerator program had us faced with the following question.

"Are you a B2B or B2C company?"

 Back before such a thing existed: "We're a B2B2C company."

<Incredulous, blank stares>

We sold to businesses but knew the data collected would have the greatest change to the individual. But the question was fundamentally asking us where we would focus our attention. Were we getting paid by businesses or were individuals getting benefit in exchange for their data that we could one day monetize? It wasn't a trivial distinction, though we thought so at the time.

Being able to focus makes a world of difference in your decision making. You're able to go faster when you give yourself and your team permission to ignore a lot of interesting opportunities because they don't fit in the narrowly defined sandbox in which you've decided you play.

Saying "no" is the best thing you can do today. Say it 99 times out of 100.

Saying "no" helps your team stay focused on the critical pieces that matter most. Too many "let's do it" nods create a whipsaw that doesn't allow the original idea to see the light of day.

While flexibility is the hallmark of a startup, it is too often its downfall as well. Your role is to keep everyone focused on producing the best product and experience possible. Every month, you'll have a hundred good ideas to do just that. But you're in the business of buying time. Every sale buys you a little more. Every round of fundraising buys you a lot.

Every new idea eats time for breakfast.

Consider These Actions:

- Know when to say yes. Tightly define the criteria that must be satisfied to give the team the green light before ever having to make that decision (e.g. what's the multiplier needed?).
- Detail the opportunity costs before making the decision. Are you willing to give up today's priority to focus on the new idea?
- Think ahead. If everything goes as planned, where does that leave the business and what additional work is generated from it?
- Write down the *one* problem you are in business to solve. Post it widely as a reminder as to where your focus must be.
- Keep the ideas. Maintain the list and revisit it periodically. Everything looks dumber (occasionally smarter) with time.

DEALING WITH IMPERFECT PRODUCTS

You know your product should be better.

You are going to reflexively apologize when showing your product in the early days. It's ugly. Its functionality is limited. It's buggy.

But.

Your product will <u>never</u> be good.

Get used to it. No amount of execution, customer surveys, or ideas will change that.

You are the reason.

You learn and generate ideas faster than any team could possibly build. Every day they improve the product, you generate a dozen ideas that will take it even further.

The frustration this causes can demoralize you. It can prevent you from charging as hard as needed into the marketplace. It can get you down on the team you've assembled, and it can leave you forgetting about the progress you've made.

The first day you look at your product and smile is the day you sell your company. Until then, you'll never be satisfied. Your dissatisfaction is critical to driving the company forward but will frustrate you endlessly.

Acknowledging your mind races faster than building occurs can help you avoid the inevitable issues. Keep those frustrations to yourself. Letting them into the wild only diminishes other teams' confidence in the product and slows the product process as motivation flags and people become fearful of making mistakes.

Consider These Actions:
*   Sales: Never apologize for your product. It's the best you can do right now, you shouldn't be apologetic for that. It will get better, but that's a reason for optimism, not skepticism.

- Support: Apologize transparently. Apologize when things don't work and be overly transparent and personal. Let the customer know which developer is working on the bug or lacking feature. Get the developer to sit in on a few calls. Introduce them to the customer who has the problem, so the challenge is personal. Customers rarely stay upset when effort and sincerity are displayed.

- Product: Good or fast? Pick one. Which bothers you more; that you are missing functionality or that the product is buggy? Align the team and create the processes to focus on the one that will make you feel better. Don't waffle. See *Having a Philosophy – Good or Fast* for more.

HAVING A PHILOSOPHY – GOOD OR FAST

You can plan for slow. You can plan for buggy. But you can't plan for random.

Product teams have a natural tension between releasing product quickly and releasing it well.

Make your choice: Good or fast?

You need a uniform philosophy—not just within your development team, but across the organization. If the game plan is known, everyone can support it.

The only requirement is consistency.

If you're a 'good' shop, you don't make promises about when a feature is being released. If you're a 'fast' shop, you set expectations upfront, so your customers know everything is a work in progress.

Both can work and customers can be happy with either when properly alerted. There are only two things that can't work. Perfect and random. The former doesn't exist, and the latter is the byproduct of weak leadership around which nobody can be accountable because things are always changing.

Consider These Actions:
- Pick a path. Align celebrations around hitting the target (good or fast) and withhold criticism if it takes too long or is too buggy, respectively.

- Set expectations. Every function should know what to expect when something new is released. They should know the resources they need to support it (e.g. other team members) and be given priority to help solve issues that arise out of the product philosophy.

- Reward the goal. Reward consistency—hitting the deadline or releasing (relatively) bug-free. It's the pattern of longer-term behavior that matters, not the result of the last release.

- Have limits. Good will have bugs and fast won't get released tomorrow. Know the range of slowness and sloppiness you want to tolerate.

BUILDING CONFIDENCE, NOT FEATURES

That first couple million in revenue is more about building confidence, than products. This is true internally and externally.

Inside your four walls, you're building confidence in one another. It's imperative your product team hit deadlines because it allows your sales team to sell in advance of where the product is today. It's crucial your account team knows how to deliver the last mile to make up for gaps in the product. And it's critical for the sales team to forecast well and produce consistently so the management team can raise funds.

Startups are a true team sport, and no more so than in the early revenue days. As the founder, it's critical that you get everyone to recognize the importance of that and to fulfill the commitments they make above everything else.

Confidence in your company is critical externally as well. Prior to any sale, your prospects need to hear that you and/or your salespeople have confidence in the product and the rest of the team. It's one of the reasons why, "it's on our roadmap" is such a terrible response. A salesperson who can't commit is both honest and lacks confidence in the product team.

After the sale, it's crucial that you build the confidence of your new customers. Most people aren't as technologically savvy as you are and will be reticent to do something wrong. They don't 'click around.' That's scary. Being there to guide them and answer questions in real time gets them feeling more comfortable using the product. The more comfortable they are, the more value they find. The more value they find, the more they recommend you to others.

Confidence has monetary value.

Every team will miss forecasts but only the product is tangible. Those tangible misses have outsized consequences on the collective confidence because the product *is* the company. The consequences of poor forecasting are rarely communicated. Take the time to explain them so feature scoring involves more than a few moments of consideration.

Consider These Actions:
* Follow through on commitments. Anyone can make a commitment; few can keep them. Building confidence amongst teams means regularly

making commitment deposits. It's hokey but consider opening up a commitment account for everyone. Following through earns a deposit. Failing to do so, a withdrawal.

- Make teammates vulnerable. Get them to express the worst part of their jobs, what it feels like to let others down, and how everyone can help them. Not foolproof, but it's hard to point fingers at another if they're already asking for help.

- Ride shotgun. When people must perform the worst parts of their jobs or when they need to communicate bad news, pair them with a counterpart. Let others feel that uncomfortableness. Sharing pain ensures nobody is a scapegoat. For example, have a developer join the call to tell a customer their request isn't ready or that a bug has created an issue with their data.

COMBATING FEATURE CREEP

Features are exponentially expensive.

The cost of a feature isn't just the time to build it. It's the time required to support it (technologically and with humans), to teach customers how to use it, to craft training videos, to teach salespeople why it's critical, as well as the unseen downstream impact it has on the rest of the code base.

Every product roadmap underprices the cost of features by focusing only on the bottleneck; the development time to create. Considering the costs borne by other teams can help slim down every product, roadmap, and feature.

There has to be a compelling reason to travel the path to add another feature before the first step is taken. The back of the envelope cost-benefit analysis has 20-80 vision, largely due to how we value the time of each of our team members.

What's said: "It'll only take two days."
What's true: It'll take two weeks, but because we rushed it, it'll have been poorly conceived, and we'll have missed several use cases. The lack of forethought puts a lot of onus on the support team to learn what it does and how to work around the pieces we missed.

What's said: "We're ready to push; let's go!"
What's true: Few people know what the feature is and why it's being released. Time hasn't been taken to update marketing materials, teach the sales team how to present it in a demo, or teach the support team the use cases for which this is most useful and how to use it.

Features are costly because they need to be fixed, improved, untangled from future features, messaged, demonstrated, and supported. With every new feature, you bear costs far beyond your development teams' time.

Wade slowly into the feature pool unless it is the defining feature that is preventing a deluge of sales. Is the new feature missing or are the existing features just not working hard enough to create value?

Consider These Actions:

- Track customer usage. It's obvious, but time is rarely invested in putting the scaffolding in place to understand which customers are using which features and why.

- Deprecate features. An interesting exercise is to rank the features you have based upon which are the least usable, most under-utilized, or that fall outside of your current scope. Loop in sales and support, too. Their perspective will most likely differ because they're closest to the customer. Even so, there will often be pretty strong agreement on the bottom one or two. Consider deprecating the universally poor ones now and schedule *unhack* time. Give some time for your product team to unhack the product. What would it save in terms of time going forward?

- Track support issues by feature so you understand which features consume the most non-development time. It's the ones that require no time at all that are interesting in this case. It either means they're flawless or unused.

BALANCING BIASES IN CUSTOMER FEEDBACK

Competing priorities inevitably create friction within and across teams. Everyone has slightly different information upon which they're basing their rationale. While there's value in the discussion, the time it consumes and angst it can create are typically a net negative.

Turning customer feedback into something profitable requires understanding the bias you have when hearing the feedback. Every role sees it slightly differently, but we're all human and subject to finding the data that confirms our viewpoint.

When everyone has a little piece of the puzzle, it looks like the whole thing from their perspective. Save time and engender focus by consolidating all the 'n of 1s' to help everyone see the whole puzzle.

There are a number of ways to solve your problem and most of them will work. Don't let the team spin too much on finding the perfect solution for the tiny piece of puzzle they see. Pick a solution that addresses a broad swatch and go. You can always improve it later.

Founder
You started this company and the product is a manifestation of what's rattling around in your brain. That is required and has its benefits, particularly if you started the company because you felt the pain as the operator who now buys your product.

But that sword's opposite edge is Ginsu sharp; you will hold your opinions far firmer and be far more likely to dismiss prospects or customers as not understanding their plight.

The challenge you must overcome is sourcing conflicting views and seeing the genius in each of them.

Product Team
It's crucial to get your product development team in front of potential customers. It helps them understand what life is like on a day-to-day basis, how savvy the customers are, and what would make the customer's job easier. But they can't be out talking to everyone; they still need to build something.

We, thus, tend to put them in front of a small handful of customers because it's better than nothing. And while true, it tends to cement thinking around one particular solution based on a memorable statement they heard.

They want to be helpful and find a great solution, but they only know how a couple of customers approach the problem, not all of them. Small '*ns*' are dangerous data points. If it doesn't translate to other customers, it's useless. The difference between zero and one is that they've now hardened their mentality around the fact that they are right.

Sometimes a little bit of knowledge is a dangerous thing. Getting product teams to recognize that is not easy but required.

Support

Working on the business end of feedback means support has the most natural and informed perspective. But, they too, bring their own bias. They hear about what's not working, but rarely about what else customers would pay more for.

Navigating the negative is a brutal job and can influence the priorities they see. The customer who yells the loudest and most frequently will often jump the queue, regardless of the value it creates for the rest of the customer base.

Sales

The same holds true for other teams. While sales have a large '*n*,' they are human and held hostage to recency bias.

Salespeople want to understand why deals fail. It's easier on their psyche when the reason is external to themselves—like a missing feature. Thus, the missing feature is the top priority in their minds because it's literally costing them compensation.

What many don't realize is that the prospects are riffing off what's in front of them, so the feedback differs when the sales approach differs. Feedback is often a reflection of what and how something is presented, rather than the content (i.e. features) itself.

Salespeople have an '*n*' of many. But they have a strong confirmation bias simply via how they present and the questions they ask.

Ultimately, nobody's view is wrong; just incomplete. To keep momentum going, you need a process to break the ties.

Consider These Actions:

- Keep a running list of 'learnings.' Put it in view of everyone and encourage everyone to grab a pen and write what they've discovered.

- Assemble a customer roundtable. Turn customers into Roman emperors who can give the thumbs up/down in order to break intractable positions.

- Choreograph conversations so team members interact with a broad cross-section of customers/prospects (e.g. by size, features used, or package purchased).

- Allow your team to shadow others for a day. Pair a product person with a salesperson, etc. Having more than a single conversation will provide a more complete picture.

- Include learning summaries in your weekly team meetings. Encourage everyone to bring the 'data' they've collected.

- Create a process to assign metrics to requests. How much time will it save the support team? How much new revenue might it generate? How many customers will it prevent from churning?

CUSTOMERS

Albert Einstein supposedly declared that compounding interest was the 8th Wonder of the World. While the attribution is dubious, the sentiment isn't.

It's close cousin, the recurring revenue model, may be Wonder #8.1. If you never lose a customer, you'll never have a down year. That's pretty incredible.

But the attention applied to retaining customers is often a fraction of the inevitable handwringing over acquiring new ones.

Managing customers is the least-appreciated function in most businesses. The subconscious belief is that the product keeps customers happy.

But few people foster relationships with software. They have relationships with people. It's people who can buy you second and third chances to recover from mistakes. It's people who build the confidence in others to use your product in the first place.

If you take care of your account managers, they'll take care of your customers. But taking care of them requires taking a thoughtful approach to the challenge and recognizing costs that aren't obvious.

If supporting customers falls squarely on you alone at the moment, now is when you put the processes and expectations in place. Get started documenting the new customer's journey so it's slightly easier to hand off when you can afford to grow the team.

If you already have a team in place, don't assume churn is a given. Every bump in retention compounds over the coming years. This makes meeting the unspoken investor mandate of 70+% growth that much closer to possible; key to showing momentum and raising follow-on money.

Resources abound about how to best support customers. But rarely is there an acknowledgement of the mental tax customers can place on a company. It's literally a cost of doing business, but it's not a fixed rate. The amount you and your teams pay is dependent upon your ability to manage expectations and recognize the costs demanded.

Supporting your customers is a thankless job that bears the brunt of the mistakes and shortcomings of others. It's the tip of the spear that breaks bad news. The negative comments pile up, while the positives are few and often only a 'thank you' for quickly resolving a negative.

But, done well, it's the backbone upon which success is found and can be a serious weapon in the battle for the next customer and the battle to extend the time left in the game.

In a world where you are trying to buy time, your account service teams are the best return on investment you'll find. They will spare you from thinking the sky is falling and, literally, buy you added days with every renewal.

GAINING ADOPTION

They bought it. Now comes the hard part: getting them to use it.

I don't care what you sell, you are in the behavior-change business. Some products require more change than others, but there isn't one that doesn't require some sort of change.

Humans use your product. Most humans find change difficult.

The more you're able to account for that in your product and in your onboarding process, the less churn you'll have. The less churn, the faster your revenue compounds.

This is a team effort and this section should be sprinkled throughout, but it's usually (incorrectly) viewed as an account management role so it resides here accordingly. But the answer to how best to get customers using your products lies with redefining the role every team plays in the process.

Sales
Sales is showing someone that the cost of using your product is way less than the benefit they get. The factors that play into each are different for every prospect, which is what makes sales so difficult.

The emotional cost to switch is the most expensive. Those costs are accrued even if the customer isn't currently using anything.

The status quo requires action. Your process requires action. The cost to switch is the difference between the two. It encompasses everything from new performance expectations placed upon your customer, the possibility of revealing years of inadequate effort, adding more unknowns into an existing job description, etc. Psychological costs far outweigh the financial costs. You know the value of a dollar. You will never know the cost associated with fear.

Change management entails walking the prospect through the change and proving that each step is as easy as the last.

Sales is the crisis negotiator.

A crisis negotiator doesn't talk straight ROI and throw calculators at the person on the ledge to prove the future is more valuable with their life in it. Instead, they work to understand the fears, concerns, and challenges that are present in that person's life. Their goal is to open the door a crack and get them to admit there may be other ways out of the situation that don't involve leaping. They show empathy and pull the thread on other ways to escape their dilemma.

The unknown will always exist, but there's no way it can be as bad as your prospect envisions. After all, people buy your product all the time and survive.

Product
Make it foolproof.

Because people who build products are more facile with technology, it's sometimes hard to empathize with people who are afraid of what will happen if they click the 'wrong' button. The difference between you and your most technophobic customers is the confidence that you can recover from making a mistake.

When you can make your product easy to use for the least-savvy customer, adoption increases. If you make it impossible for someone to look foolish, you can convince them to try something new.

Remember, your customer knew the process of how to complete the same task before you arrived. If they always followed the same path, then there was no opportunity to make a mistake. They knew that path. It may be long, muddy, and filled with thorny bushes, but it was familiar. They knew where every thorn was and could navigate around them with minimal scratches.

Your product? It's risk with a nicer user interface. Your assurance that there are no thorny bushes is meaningless. Your least tech-savvy customers know from experience, not by trusting someone who explains how to navigate your product too quickly and who doesn't understand the cost of screwing up.

Change management via product development is a function of building something where even the most timid knows what will happen when every button is clicked.

You're in the confidence game. Every time they click, and the product does what they expected, you make a single confidence deposit. If something unexpected occurs, then you may not have banked enough deposits to endure.

Confidence breeds use. Usage breeds revenue.

Support
Be overly involved.

Onboarding is the most critical piece of customer interaction and enacting change.

It's the first time that customers experience your product in action and their first experience working with your team as a partner. It's the point at which the risk is highest for your new customer and when churn risk is highest for you.

The habits you shape early will set the expectations for usage down the road. Those expectations, when met, lead to renewals.

Those first few months can be scary for your customer. They are still on the hook for producing the same results but are doing so with a different process (and perhaps still using the old process just in case).

Teaching everyone how to use your product isn't enough. You need to use it with them. Onboarding can be a breeding ground for confidence. You are successful when they walk away and know how to do what they need to do.

Hearing the step-by-step while half paying attention and checking their social-media feeds isn't going to cut it. Your success is their action, not their attendance. Get in there with them on the day they need to pull the report your product generates. Listen to them hunt for the right keys and deliberate what dates they need to enter.

If you're there for them on day one, it will set the hook for them using it themselves on day two.

Consider These Actions:
- You can't overdo in-product metrics. Your support team should get daily reports of all new customers' use patterns in order to proactively reach out and get them through the next phase. You won't lose an account by contacting someone too often. You will if you don't anticipate their trepidation and let them flail for too long without you.
- Account for your customer's employee turnover. Every time a new employee takes over ownership of using your product, you run the risk of churn. Onboarding is required for every new user, not just when the sale is inked. Without monitoring use and tracking new users, the first time you hear of the onboarded employee is when they want to cancel. Get in front

of that and prevent it from happening by knowing usage patterns so you can reach out when patterns change.

- Create bite-sized onboarding. Ignoring someone on a conference call is too easy. Ignoring a webinar is even easier. It's like a free hour to do personal internet reading while your colleagues think you're busy. Break your onboarding process up into bite-sized chunks to maximize retention (the information kind) and to make the most efficient use of your time and theirs. Repeat often.

FINDING FEEDBACK - USAGE TRACKING

Why does usage tracking always slide down the roadmap?

It makes obvious sense to understand what your customers are using within your product, but we rarely spend enough time laying the groundwork to vigilantly track it.

We rely on anecdotal evidence rather than concrete usage statistics because the latter comes at the cost of building new features. New features sell, and it pacifies the screaming voice in our head that tells us how inferior our product is to the competition's.

But there's an unseen cost to forgoing the foundational elements of how people engage with the very thing that generates revenue. This is one of those rare cases where the upfront cost of implementing *is* paid back exponentially down the road.

Aside from resolving opinion-driven debate, there are critical, revenue-related reasons to implement in-product usage tracking. Namely:

Pricing - Identifying the right price to charge and creating proper tiers is never easy. Data that show you how your customers are using the product will illuminate where they find value. When value is known, it makes it easier to bundle features and set pricing tiers.

Churn - Churn is the dagger that slays your exponential growth. Usage tracking can help you get smart in predicting who is most likely to stop paying. Knowing who needs your support and where to apply the efforts of the account management team is like doubling your salesforce without adding headcount.

Efficiency - Shrinking product and firing customers can and should be done. Bigger isn't always better. 'Bigger' is more to support, more bugs to fix, and more internal debate about where to focus next. Knowing what is being used allows you to shrink your product and/or 'fire' vocal edge-case customers who pull your focus away from the bulk of the revenue base.

Consider These Actions:
* Automate everything today. The amount of time it takes to track is minimal in the grand scheme of building a product. You'll never regret

knowing too much, nor will you miss the week that was spent building the foundation.

- Roll product-use analytics into product and support meetings. Use is the only guarantee of continued revenue and will help everyone see their impact on the company's top line.
- Make non-use visible. Create a public, running list of those customers who are churn risks due to their lack of use. The more visible you make the invisible, the more attention it gets.

MANAGING CUSTOMER COMPLAINTS

There will be weeks when you feel like you can't do anything right for your customer. When that happens, remember: *You* are not your product. It's critical you disassociate yourself with it so you can hear feedback and encourage your team.

Hearing someone call your baby ugly is always painful.

Many founders, because they define themselves by their product and vice versa, take it personally. In those cases, it is a criticism of their intelligence, vision, or the job they're doing. That challenges you in every way possible.

That's normal. It's also a good thing. Really. It means people are using the product and they care that it's not working. Without caring, there is no renewal.

Here's an example: After four years of building, selling, and servicing his product, a founder I advised couldn't stand talking to his customers any longer. Every time he picked up the phone, he learned of another bug or missing feature. After literally being the face of the company, the complaints created a negative mental soundtrack.

He picked up the phone less frequently, abdicated responsibility for talking to customers onto others, and complained about his teams' shortcomings. It was a vicious cycle whereby he was stressed about the issues because he didn't want to lose customers (revenue), but the further he withdrew and the more he cast blame, the more likely he was to lose those customers.

It affected his relationships, internally and externally. He wasn't the same person around whom people wanted to spend time. He didn't have the inclination to lead and assigned the company's problems to his employees' rather than himself. That type of leader only inspires the weak.

The founder became a motivational anchor. While delegating the responsibility of supporting customers is the right thing to do, it exacerbated his stress because he clung to the notion that customers were still buying him. (They weren't. The team had done a great job of creating value on their own and new customers had no idea who he was.). But admitting that would have started the process of questioning the value he brought. (There was plenty, but he couldn't rewrite his own job description to play to his strengths and identify the things that energized him.)

While the company still grew, the employees were leaving at 5 p.m. on the dot. Effort flagged, but inertia reigned long enough to sell for a 'lifestyle' price. The founder's original vision of what could have been was lost and the generational wealth he sought along with it. The footnote is that the competition reclaimed the leadership position and went on to raise a large round of funding a couple years later with a valuation deep into the eight figures.

Supporting customers requires that you support yourself and those who care for them. You need to mentally separate yourself from your product. Even if you are required in order to make every sale, you can't touch every customer every day and still maintain your own sanity.

Give yourself permission to let bugs be bugs rather than a condemnation on your intelligence, skills, or intentions. Be attentive, but only so much so that you retain the energy to inspire and lead the rest of the team, too.

Consider These Actions:
If you're the tip of the spear:

- Proactively pick up the phone to call your customers. You're far more likely to hear the positive if you catch them on your time rather than when things are wrong.

- Write your job description based on your stage and the next. Give yourself permission to define your success based on all functions of your role, not just what the last customer said.

- Ask for help. Before it's taken everything out of you, ask your co-founder or someone else to take over for a bit. Not only will it build appreciation for the job you've done, but it will give you a needed break.

If you have a team:

- Take in the feedback but promise nothing yourself. Ensure your support lead responds with details of the commitments. Facilitate the connection to solve the problem rather than solving it yourself.

- Trust your team leads to prioritize. Resist the urge to ride roughshod over the roadmap because an early customer reached out directly with an issue. Your word never loses its gravitas internally unless you start reactively blowing up priorities without full knowledge of the alternatives.

CONVERTING FREE BETAS

When should you ask your betas to pay?

Nine times in ten, the answer should be "on day one." But some industries and competitive situations call for unpaid pilots; like when price tags are high, when one or two competitors own most of the market, in industries where customers are afraid of their own shadow, etc.

At some point, you need to get paid, however.

The fear is always that you'll lose a customer by asking for money.

Losing a customer validates that nagging skepticism in your head, giving you an excuse to avoid the conversation for as long as possible. But better to know now that you don't have a business than to keep slogging away and wasting time and money. If that pessimistic point of view is too dire, then you can, at least, learn what you need to create to get someone to pay.

Until someone is forced to make a decision with an associated cost, everything is theoretical. Without a cost, feedback is unproductive. Anything that adds value is valuable. That doesn't necessarily mean it's worth paying for, just that more free stuff is good. Only fools say "no" to more for free.

Forcing betas to pay is the only way to understand what you have and where you're falling short. You incur a cost with every customer, whether it's monetary, time-based, or lost opportunities. The difference between a business and a hobby is getting money in return for the cost you bore.

Get started. Do not e-mail. Pick up the phone. They won't be happy to hear it's time to pay, but you need to get as much feedback as possible. That includes hearing how upset they are with the decision, how they respond to the actual price, and what they're going to do if they replace your product.

Start with the customer you dislike. The worst thing that can happen is that you lose someone who was willing to give your product a try but who was also trying your patience.

Your first call will be halting, awkward, and will likely come out wrong. Plan on it. There is a price for being rude or overbearing, make them pay it. Make your mistakes here since you lose less should they walk.

Consider These Actions:

- Play unafraid. You will lose customers. Losing one when you only have a few is difficult because you still crave that validation. But know you will get others. And don't fear asking for money because it's the only way to build your business. Don't be afraid of asking for a lot. Ultimately, if nobody laughs at your price or swears at you, you're not charging enough.

- Play the psychological game. If you're nervous about throwing out the first number because you have no idea if it's in the ballpark, ask your beta what they think their customers would pay. It has the benefit of getting them out of their own budget and thinking about someone who they want to pay more than they themselves would.

- Make payment conditional. You need to get paid; betas need certain value. If there's something missing where they aren't completely getting what they need, then craft an agreement where payment begins after a certain time period, when that gap is filled, or offer a money-back guarantee. Nothing motivates a product team to finish a feature faster than the prospect of the product generating revenue.

PREVENTING CHURN - SHITBURGER AVOIDANCE

The person who buys your product is often not the one who uses it. In servicing your customers, you are thus serving two masters—the user and the one who foots the bill. It's a tough spot to be in and one that requires you understand the challenges each face.

You've convinced the one holding the checkbook of the value you bring, but your job now is to make sure the end user is using the product and that they have no issues with it.

What will wind up killing these kinds of deals is when the end user repeatedly complains to the buyer (often their manager) about the software not making sense, being too difficult to use, too buggy, or too time-consuming.

Every time your end user complains, they add another shitburger to your buyer's desk.

At some point, no matter how little faith the buyer has in their employee or how much value they know you bring, they are going to want to clear the desk of all the shitburgers and go back to operating the way they had been.

Customer success is a shitburger-prevention business. You need to bend over backward to keep the end user feeling intelligent and confident about your product.

The smarter someone feels when using your product, the more they'll use it.

Unfortunately, the reverse is true in spades. When people don't get it, the downside of looking bad is enormous. Nobody wants to put their livelihood on the line for you. Instead of taking the time to learn your product, it's easier to trash it and make sure everyone is well aware of how little value provided.

Your account managers' role is to take away all opportunities for someone to crap on your product. That begins with building the user's confidence as soon as they log in and showing them how to extract value when they use it.

If you have customers who 'don't get it' or seem to endlessly complain, share your screen and do their job for them. An hour now can avoid the days to re-sell after their boss' desk has been swept clean of shitburgers.

Consider These Actions:

- Proactively fill the silence. When people aren't using your product and they aren't reaching out for help, you know you have a problem. Harass your customers to use your product. That starts by understanding what's happening on the ground with them and helping them fit your product into their workflow. Call them.

- Keep an open line of communication with the buyer. Get them to understand how much you're trying to engage the end user and ask what else you can do. The buyer knows her employee's limitations. Your job is to paper over their weaknesses, not highlight them.

- Use your product to speak for you. Alerts are annoying, but effective. Send push alerts and e-mails when a user isn't logging in. Give them multiple opportunities to reach out for help and continually remind them of the value you can provide.

PREVENTING CHURN - BE THE IDIOT

It's probably not your fault. But take the blame anyway.

You need to understand what you're selling. Sometimes the value is obvious based on what gets spit out the other end of your product. Other times, it's just air cover.

You can make or break someone's performance review. That's a serious responsibility. For that reason, you need to be willing to jump into the line of fire when your customer's manager is looking for heads to put on a stick.

Vendors can be risk mitigators for individual employees. They become an easy outlet at which the fingers can be pointed when things go wrong.

You are being paid to be a scapegoat. It won't always be your fault, but there is little to be gained by illuminating the user error that led to the point where you have to step in.

Most managers know the limitations of their team members. You don't have to highlight them further. It just makes you look petty and fosters distrust. After all, if you're willing to throw the subordinate under the bus with their manager then you'd do the same to that manager's manager.

There is nothing lost by accepting responsibility and committing to double down on training or extracting the value from the product yourself. It implicitly says, "your employee doesn't have any idea what he's doing," in a way that assumes responsibility and shows you're willing to work hard to correct the issue.

Some people need to be able to point the finger and say, "that guy is the idiot." Keep in mind that you're not just selling a product, you're selling an excuse.

Consider These Actions:
- Take the heat. Become the scapegoat so your account team members don't have to. Your job is also to protect your own employees, so they want to keep showing up and putting their best feet forward. By taking the heat yourself, you provide your team the same air cover as you do the customer. Model the behavior you seek.

- Communicate with your account team. Help them know that by accepting responsibility on behalf of your customer, they aren't admitting to you that they've done a bad job. Make the ability to be a scapegoat a part of their reward system so they don't feel a need to be defensive when a customer's finger is pointed their way.
- Offer up your presence. Join your customer in a meeting where the output of your product is the topic du jour. Highlight how you believe the product can help and take the blame for not bringing that value to the fore earlier. Manually go the last mile so your buyer looks great in front of his or her peers.

PREVENTING CHURN - CONTRACT TIMING

Annual or multi-year contracts are wonderful, but there is a downside. With a contract comes an active decision point. Every time a conscious decision is required, the value of your product will be questioned.

There are so many things that are out of your hands when renewals are due; employee turnover at your customer's company, changing political winds within their four walls, financial fires that demand clear cutting all non-headcount expenses, or any number of personal issues that are interfering with your end users' ability to do their job.

But churn is SaaS' kryptonite. You have to stack the deck as much as possible to favor the renewal in order to grow exponentially.

One often-overlooked tool at your disposal that can absolutely increase your retention a couple points is how you structure contracts. Specifically, the timing of the renewal relative to when the customer sees value, has money, or is likely dealing with bigger fish. Consider:

Adjusting to Customer Cash Flow
If your customers have lumpy cash flow, where they're rolling in it during one point of the year and struggling another, you're better off requesting the renewal when times are good and the hit to their cash account is relatively small.

Distillery Solutions sold to distillers, most of whom spent their budget building up inventory and pushing product out of their shop in Q4. They wouldn't see the cash from their distributors until Q1, however.

While our product was critical to their business at all times of year, the decision to renew was a lot easier when the decision wasn't forcing them to choose between making holiday payroll and buying raw materials or paying for our software. After cash had been collected from distributors, they were able to take a more objective look at the value provided for the cost. It left us drafting 16-month contracts if someone closed in September or saying no payments were due for the first four months so that most renewals happened in February.

Aligning with Customer Chaos
You don't need to be nefarious but aligning renewal decisions around times when your customers tend to be preoccupied with bigger decision points is a path to consider.

For example, youth sports registration is an incredibly competitive market—to the point where there is now a free offering from a big-box retailer just so they can promote buying equipment from them.

But legacies die hard. While serving on the board of our local Little League, I saw this come into play every year. The registration vendor we used set us up for renewal every October. Little League's governing body states that local leagues must recruit new board members and hold elections—you guessed it—every September in order to start a new year in October.

Changing out half the board takes time and occurs when the decision point should be made to switch to the free option. But those who remain engaged after the season ends have their hands full elsewhere. Renewals, despite the sizeable expense to a non-profit, happen because of timing, not a critical evaluation of the ROI.

Aligning to Value
A portion of those who churn will do so because they can't justify the cost. It could mean they aren't using your product properly, that budgets are tight, *or* it could mean that the value they've gotten recently doesn't outweigh the cost. They are victims of recency bias.

To counter this, align contract renewals around the times when your customers are extracting peak value. Doing so allows the recency bias to work in your favor and cover for those periods when the value is on par or lower than the costs. It also increases switching costs as they need to plan ahead and get something new in place prior to entering their high-value period.

The timing of revenue may not be ideal for you, but retention itself is always ideal.

Consider These Actions:
- Identify the frequency of your value points. The more frequently you provide a critical function, the less likely you are to need contracts. Contracts present decision points. If your value is seasonal, establish contracts to renew in the midst of the season or immediately following. You know when you're most valuable to your customers. Align renewals around those times.

- Know everyone's renewal date. You should have a list of when each customer is set to renew so you can plot the course to maximize value in the months leading up to the renewal date. Recency bias is a real thing and you need to use it to your advantage. You can't start this process with 30 days to go. You need to start three or four months in advance if they are actively using the product, longer if not.

- Align renewal to cash flow. Some industries have cyclical cash flow and you fight a stiff headwind, regardless of the value you provide, when you ask for money when there is none to be had. Whether it's to align with fiscal year budgets, cash flow considerations, or excessively busy times, you have to find the time that works best for your customers. You don't care when they renew so long as they do.

- Communicate and educate. Your customer has no idea of the improvements you've made and the new functionality that exists. They have too many other things to do and aren't reading your monthly updates. Get your account team on a cycle where they're calling a few customers each day to, likely, leave a voicemail about the latest feature or identify an area where the customer may get more value.

FIRING CUSTOMERS

Not all customers are worth having. There are times when you need to fire one.

Some things are worth more than money and firing a customer can have long-term benefits that you can't yet see.

The decision to fire a customer is never easy, however. You worked hard to acquire them after all.

And, in fairness, not all difficult customers are worth expelling. But not all are worth keeping either and you need to know the difference.

Some occasions when firing a customer may be worthwhile:

Opportunity Costs of Complaints
Some people like to feel important and will make highly unreasonable requests that are out of bounds from what you're hearing from every other customer or what you've sold.

If there isn't value in their complaints, consider freeing up several hours of your account team's time each week. You'll keep your team happy and come out ahead in the long run.

Basic Human Decency
If a customer isn't treating your people with respect and you are constantly hearing the team grouse, then it is well worth understanding why. You may find that it's not because your team isn't doing their job, but because the person on the other end of the line is a miserable jerk, taking out their frustrations on your team.

Fire the jerk. Often, bullies need to be punched in the nose and have their bad behavior called out before they stop. Occasionally, by calling the bully on their antics, you'll earn their respect and future business. If not, you eliminate a major emotional drain on your team.

Mis-Sold Customers
Sometimes what is said in the sales process isn't interpreted as it was intended. It could be a salesperson wanting to close a deal or the prospect hearing what

they want to hear. But miscommunication will happen, and expectations won't be properly set, thus opening the door to a contentious on-going relationship.

If someone isn't getting what they thought they were sold, cut bait. You aren't likely to bridge the functionality gap any time soon and the little revenue they generate will be more than eaten up by their bad-mouthing you to anyone who will listen or taking out their frustrations on the support team.

In the beginning, all revenue is like the air you breathe after being stuck underwater for too long. But that mentality can create demoralizing situations or distractions (if they push the roadmap in a direction you didn't intend).

Know the difference between those situations and when you're simply taking your lumps from hard-to-please customers because they're pushing you forward and making you better.

Firing a customer is just admitting a mistake was made bringing them aboard. Nobody works error-free.

Consider These Actions:

- Know 100% won't renew. Of the 10-20% who won't renew, feel comfortable being the first to offer to part ways. The financial justification comes from increasing the likelihood you retain the remainder.

- Know when to push back...hard. Despite everything said earlier about being a scapegoat, there are times when it's worth fighting. If you are sticking up for your employees, allowing them to overhear your fighting on their behalf has far more downstream value than any revenue ever would.

- Level expectations early in the onboarding process and confirm the problems the customer wants to solve. Create a communication trail. Honest mistakes will be forgiven, but people get angry when they feel intentionally misled.

SALES

Odds are that you founded your company because you wanted autonomy.

Some part of your professional life wouldn't be satisfied until you could do things your way. Someone else was profiting from your ideas, the rules governing your day didn't jibe with you, or you knew you could solve a problem better than everyone currently trying.

The road to autonomy is paved in sales.

Even after taking outside investment, it is only monthly revenue growth that can buy you operational freedom. Strong sales buy you time to overcome inevitable missteps and allow you to invest in the areas you see fit.

So, start selling. It's never too early.

Are you apprehensive because you've never done it before?

That's understandable, but the best way to learn is to start doing it. Selling is a skill and has nothing to do with what a personality test tells you. Fortunately, all skills can be learned. It just takes practice and the belief that a 'no' today isn't a 'no' forever.

Are you repulsed by the image of what salespeople are like?

Don't be. That stereotype is wrong. Convincing people to buy something they don't want is not what makes successful salespeople. You don't have to be extroverted, highly charismatic, or willing to be a charlatan, you just have to be human and believe in your product.

Are you scared of being rejected?

Completely fair, almost everyone is. But you proved capable of putting your fears aside by executing when you started the company. Do it again. Your future demands it.

Do you think there are more important priorities that must be addressed first?

Well, here we'll disagree. You're just wrong. Your employees can't pay rent with product features. Your vendors don't work in exchange for improvements to the marketing website. If your goal isn't to build a product, but to build a company, then you need to find revenue every day.

Selling isn't the reason many founders start a company so it's easy to excuse the lack of attention to the topic. On your framed cocktail napkin, I guarantee the drawing isn't of what the sales process looks like. The solution makes your company real to you. Sales make your company real to the rest of the world. Without sales, the lights are shut off and your solution collects dust on some digital shelf. Without sales, the clock speeds to 0:00 awfully quickly.

It's never too early to change your relationship to the sales process. For some, it just takes enough knowledge to get started and a lot of practice. For others, it takes reframing how they think about the function.

I've made countless mistakes. First, I lost my autonomy. Then, my company. I hope the suggestions that follow help speed you on your journey to buying the time and autonomy a repeatable sales model brings.

One final thought:

The best advice I've ever gotten was to <u>never</u> use the words 'sales' and 'easy' in the same sentence. As a first-time founder who had never sold anything previously, I didn't appreciate this until the umpteenth deal that I was *sure* would close fell through. There is no such thing as an easy sale. Believing so will only make you (or, worse, your sales team) look bad when something inevitably comes up that thwarts pen hitting paper.

REFRAMING WHAT IT MEANS TO SELL

Sales is too often a verb.

You '*do*' sales, whereas she *is* a developer. Because we think of it as a verb, we think offensively. We have to be pushing, talking, *selling*! If sales were a martial art, it'd be of the mixed martial-art variety—constantly attacking.

The reality is that sales is a verb right up to the point when you are granted an audience.

Everyone has slightly different needs, slightly different motivations; and buying committees have different dynamics.

Until you hear their unique needs, motivations, and internal dynamics, however, you can't help them. You can guess and just start pitching your demo deck (singular), but why would you when you could just ask them?

Listening allows you to respond to people with what they need to hear rather than what you want to say. Nuance is critical to winning. Going on the offensive requires you get lucky and strike the right note. Listening and reacting to what they have to say allows them to tell you which note is correct and the one for which they're willing to pay.

Sales isn't mixed martial arts, it's simply judo. Judo requires you be nimble and have the moves in your repertoire to use the prospect's momentum as the force to change, no matter where it's aimed.

Your job as a salesperson is to unlock information that you can then use to close. Take control of your sales process. But know the one leading is the one asking questions, not the one talking.

Consider These Actions:
- Find a sales mentor. This is especially true if you've never sold before. Sales is one of the least intuitive areas of the business and one where a part-time consultant can be particularly valuable.
- Do it. It's a slog. Make the 25+ calls a day. Hear 'no' dozens of times. Keep following through with someone who said they were interested but won't return your call. Do all the hard things that make you want to just pawn sales off on someone else. You will be in a better position to support

your sales team when you understand how hard the job is and how to overcome the pain.

- Spend as much time with your sales team as you do with your product team. Your focus is always on what's in front of you. If you sit with the sales team, eavesdrop on conversations, gather feedback, hear their challenges, etc. You'll be far more likely to empathize and dig in to help.

SELLING AN IMPERFECT PRODUCT

You will never be satisfied with your product. In the beginning you'll actually be appalled. It will be ugly. It will be broken. It will be missing obvious features that you know you need.

You'll want to apologize. You'll want to make excuses.

Don't.

Don't apologize, not out of arrogance or an unwillingness to show weakness, but because it demonstrates a lack of confidence. If you aren't confident in your product, your prospect can't be either.

Sales is hard enough when you're implicitly asking prospects to trust you to do right by them. It's almost impossible when you don't trust yourself.

Your product is what it is. Even if it's not good, it's the best you have available to you right now. If you've done your best, why are you apologizing?

Apologizing tells your prospects that it's not ready yet. It is the verbal acknowledgment of the risk your prospect will be taking on. Why not just wait until it is ready?

Instead, focus on the value and the one thing it solves right now. If something gives people what they need, then the look is secondary. If you click a button and get an error page, move on. It happens to fully baked software too.

Get comfortable with your product always being 60% of what you think it should be. It'll never get better than that because your knowledge of the space and the ideas you generate will always outpace how quickly your team can translate them into new features.

Failing to acknowledge areas where you can improve is dangerous, but it should be done within the four walls of your office, not in front of prospects, and certainly not in the midst of a demo.

Consider These Actions:
* Write down the problem you solve before every call or presentation. Sure, it's hokey, but it's a reminder that you're doing something right.

- Take ten-minutes to prepare before every demo. Run through the product and workflow prior to presenting. A lack of preparation leads to panic and reflexive apologies when the unexpected is encountered.
- If it looks bad, focus on the value. If it looks good, focus on the value. Focus on a list of success stories, regardless of whether the you're bridging the last mile manually or not.

EXTRACTING VALUE BEYOND REVENUE

When does it make sense to charge a dollar for something that costs you two to produce?

This was an argument my co-founder and I had all the time. Because neither of us changed our positions, we were both right. He over the first couple of years, me over the successive years.

In the beginning, it's a must. The difference between your costs to fulfill the promise made to a customer and your revenue is simply a marketing cost. But there are a number of things that have tremendous value to you that you can ask for in return. The cost to your customer? Nothing.

You don't want to start believing that the price those early customers are paying is what your product is worth. It's not. The price reflects your product's value minus the perceived risk taken by the customer. As you gain customers, the perceived risk should fall over time. You'll have learned on someone else's dime so your rollout will be smoother, adoption will be quicker, bugs will be fewer, etc.

There is always a way to make a deal happen if you're willing to be creative. Identifying non-monetary pieces of value and adding those to a deal can help bridge the value-risk gap and make the relationship valuable to you both.

The key is following through on them and making sure your customer is doing what she promised.

Acknowledge this and hold the price you charge loosely (but only in the beginning). There are always ways you can extract value from your customer without adding financial cost.

Here are some examples in the likely order of value to you:

Case study
The case study requires the sharing of your customers data with you. Outline the data you will need from them so you can find a story to show the value.

Don't lock yourself into what that story is in the beginning because it may come from a completely unexpected source. Get pre-approved to create the story and collect the data upfront. Your interests are aligned with your buyer, so don't feel like this is a big ask. Your case study should make them look like a genius. The only hurdle on their end is whether they must go through their legal department.

Phone Calls

You will have investors and future customers who are going to need to talk to people who have used your product. Plan for those requests now by asking for their reference with every deal.

Asking a customer for their recommendation once is easy, but when the fifth or fifteenth request comes through, you're going to hesitate because you've leaned on that customer so much. Get approval for the first 15 calls upfront. Then you're simply left with alerting rather than asking.

Prepare your contact by providing a short list of talking points that you think will be important. Again, you want them to be authentic, but you can make their life easier by doing the thinking for them upfront and giving them guardrails. Doing so provides the additional benefit of repeating the same value points you've made in the sales process, but this time reiterated by someone neutral.

Testimonial

Getting your point of contact to film a 60-second video is easier than you'd think. It doesn't need to be highly produced. Ask them to turn their mobile phone around when they have a few minutes in their day. You're looking to extract their kind words and authenticity. Anyone can put a quote on a website (do that, too) but seeing the face of an actual buyer/user takes it to a whole different level.

Note: if you do ask for a testimonial quote, make it easy. Write out exactly what you'd want them to say about your product and ask them to approve it or give them the option of saying something in their own words.

Logos

Logo collecting for the website is nice, but often falls outside of your contact's ability to approve. The logo is usually owned by someone in legal or on the brand team. Getting those people to say yes is not worth the return on your time.

In fact, this is one of those cases where you want to ask forgiveness, not permission. If you are truly working with someone and they are paying you, then you can truthfully say, both verbally and on the website, that you're working with them. Don't worry today about the 'cease and desist' letter you may receive tomorrow. It's just people doing their job. They need to tick the box that they sent the letter, they don't truly care that you used the logo.

Consider These Actions:

- Always ask for value in return. Have it in writing (via e-mail, not necessarily in the contract to avoid getting bogged down with their lawyers).

- Do the legwork. Have a list of questions you anticipate people receiving, roughly outlined responses, and a couple of key messages you'd love them to reiterate.

- Hold the line on agreements. Follow through with your customer. Make sure you're getting the value you need. Don't be afraid of reminding them of their obligation.

- Know when is enough. After a number of customers are willing to field phone calls on your behalf or provide data or testimonials, you need to review your pricing. It's easy to fall into the trap of selling for X and trading for something of value, but the value of non-monetary payments diminishes with each new customer. Don't keep selling for X plus a quote when 1.5 or 2X is out there.

PRIORITIZING SALES YESTERDAY

You're not selling today because you're scared to look bad. I get it.

You don't want to waste your one shot, the thinking goes. The reality is you nearly always get a second and third opportunity if you ask.

Timing will never feel right to approach your prospects.

If wasting a bullet on a potential customer is truly damning to your business, then you're in the wrong market. It's way too small. If you aren't out there trying to push your product or to raise money, then you're not learning about what to say and where to focus.

Creating a viable company and finding traction is a function of putting yourself out there. You can tinker all day long and make things legitimately better, but you won't know if you're on the right path until you talk to someone with money on the line. They'll let you know with either a check or a 'get back to us when you have [xyz].'

Catch yourself any time you start thinking, "if we only had…" As soon as you have it, you'll wish you had something else too. 'If we only had…' is an excuse.

Only after the fact will you know if the timing was right. But by putting yourself out there, you open yourself up for new opportunities and you do so earlier. Earlier is cheaper.

Every deal takes more than one shot to close. You need to build a relationship over multiple conversations.

This is true when both selling your product or selling equity in your company.

Prospects
Any sales cycle that requires a conversation requires more than a day. If you don't have that one feature you need or if the product doesn't go the last mile yet, that's okay. You have time to lay the track before prospects sign.

The process of winning over your prospects is one of following through in order to earn their trust. That means providing materials they're unlikely to read, taking calls with their boss or boss's boss, or looping in your development team to answer technical questions.

It's a process that can take a while. Waiting until you have that one right feature completed means you're losing months of sales. By the time you navigate the prospect's organization and checked all the boxes, you'll make sure you're ready enough. And if you aren't, simply schedule the onboarding process far enough in the future to ensure you will be.

Consider These Actions:

- Make contact with at least two new prospects every day.

- Work backward from the sale. How long does each step take? What's needed from you to advance to the next stage? Show yourself that it's a long road in order to eliminate the concern that somebody will want to use your product tomorrow. It will help you get started today.

- Use the pressure of you selling to your advantage. Meaningful deadlines make things happen. Set realistic expectations and be willing to admit to a prospect you need more time, but the deadline to onboard real revenue can be a big internal motivator to meet deadlines.

FORECASTING FROM THE DETAILS

Det er vanskeligt at spaa, især naar det gælder Fremtiden.
– Danish aphorism

That translates to something close to, '[forecasts] are hard to make, especially about the future.' This is doubly true early on in your company when data is limited, and optimism is boundless.

But there is nothing more critical than hitting your plan. Investors give you a pass the first time you miss, eyebrows rise the second, and then your credibility is toast after the third.

Without investors' trust, they become anchors for the next round of funding. They may come in with their pro rata, but even if they can only write small checks, they should be sending signals of wanting to do more. Signals are crucial.

Your sales forecasts must be gold. Like setting goals with the team, it should be something you can hit 90% of the time. Sharing your projections isn't a fundraising pitch. You're not trying to convey optimism with your sales projections, you're trying to prove you understand the business.

It requires a sober, bottom-up analysis of what's probable (not what's possible) given your sales process and the cycle required to close.

The following mentalities are mistakes I've seen, and been guilty of, that erode that trust. Your credibility is all you have. Guard it ruthlessly.

"Growing XX% should absolutely be possible."
Without understanding how leads are generated, how long they marinate, and how often your team is successful, you're basically a random number generator. Wishing never makes it so.

This is true at any stage. A VP of Sales recently vented his frustration over a discussion he had with his CEO about the VP's submitted forecasts. The abridged (and sanitized) version was:

"We agreed on the strategy, so how can you now say hitting the 25% growth target is not possible?"

The VP of Sales countered, "That strategy called for generating leads through [xyz] marketing process. That process isn't even on the CMO's quarterly objectives and we have a 12-month sales cycle."

For a company historically in the high single digits, 25% growth was a fine goal, but one that required a new strategy. Everyone acknowledged that.

But making more sales requires more than trying harder. Every sale has a long list of prerequisites that must be hit. Failing to hit those means you fail to hit the target. You can't close leads what don't yet exist.

"We just need to close one or two big deals."

Focusing on elephants can be a good and profitable strategy, but it requires a lot of time to pan out.

Too often, especially early, elephant hunting is a Hail Mary. It's desirable because it seems easier. It's basically saying, "with one elephant, we can eat for the year." It takes a single bullet. Anyone can get lucky with a single bullet. And it really only takes a day. That's the subconscious thinking.

It's harder to hunt hundreds of smaller targets each month knowing that only a few will be bagged.

Complicating the approach is that elephant hunting requires a sophistication that is often out of reach for most startups.

It's not impossible. But everything must be tailored to the large enterprise. Your approach must fit your product, which must fit your customer's process and budget, which must fit pricing, which must fit your sales infrastructure, etc.

There's no room for ambiguity.

Everything must scream, "We only sell to companies exactly like yours.' Ambiguity introduces risk. Elephants don't buy risk.

"We just need a couple of channel partners."

Channel sales are similar to hunting elephants, but more appealing. You don't even have to touch the gun. There are no cold calls needed and you only hear about the wins, rarely the hard 'no.'

It's not a strategy to rule out offhand, but it's a strategy that should be approached with caution.

You'll spend a lot of time and energy doing things that don't get you closer to your goals. The requests from your partner will be numerous, even before the first sale. Product roadmaps will be tweaked without any customer feedback. Collateral will be created without direct conversation with your prospects. Channels keep you one step removed from your end user so the feedback you hear is often filtered through the bias of another.

Ultimately, you can't rely on others to sell your product until you know how to sell it yourself. Nobody wants to learn how to sell your offering on their own dime. They want the playbook that they can put in the hands of their sales reps and not have to worry about it threatening other potential sales.

Consider These Actions:

- Track everything. Ensure all points in the sales process are well defined. Bad data is worse than no data. Have strict definitions for what it means for a prospect to be qualified for each stage. For example, 'proposal out' means the prospect requested a proposal, not that you sent them one. Similarly, a lead isn't generated when they raise their hand, but only after you speak with them. Definitions matter, timing matters, and uniformity matters.

- Start selling today. The information you pick up will improve your knowledge of what it takes to sell, how long it takes, and what type of hires will best find success. You will also forecast better having done the job.

- Draw concentric rings around your targets. Those who've bought already had a higher risk tolerance. The next round of sales will come from those with slightly lower risk tolerances. Being able to bucket your targets by type will allow you to forecast with a blended win rate and time to close that accounts for the differences each present. Perhaps there aren't massive differences but accounting for them may just be enough to ensure you hit your numbers.

CREATING A REPEATABLE SALES PROCESS

Repeatable sales are the holy grail that buys you autonomy. With repeatable sales, you can raise money, cash flow the business, or get acquired. Repeatable sales are the engine whereby you know when your next demo is coming, roughly how many of those demos lead to proposals, and how many you'll win.

But cracking the code can be overwhelming because there are so many leaky holes in the sales funnel.

Try just creating repeatable leads.

Every sale starts with a lead. Repeatable sales start with repeatable lead generation.

Creating an efficient funnel is a long-term project. Until you have enough people entering through the top that you stop thinking about each of them by first name, you'll never be willing to experiment because each is too precious.

Generating leads also has benefits well beyond revenue.

It grants you the confidence of certitude. You *will* get another chance. If your product isn't right for this prospect, it will be for the next. You won't chase, you won't waste time out of pure desperation, and you won't be quite so willing to customize your product.

The best use of your time today is to find ways to generate leads. Generate them any way possible. In the beginning, it doesn't matter if they're horribly expensive or take longer than you'd like. It's about finding as many channels as possible, not about finding which are most valuable (yet).

Counting stats, not rates, matter early. Right now, every lead provides intelligence, even if it's without revenue. You need live fire (almost) regardless the price.

If you do nothing else today, do one thing that might generate a lead.

Consider These Actions:
- Buy contact information. Invest in knowing how to reach your prospects. If list brokers are too expensive, too shady, or the quality too poor, look

for manual methods to source contacts. Sites offering access to inexpensive, overseas freelancers are plentiful and the work is quite good. A thousand dollars spent here may seem like a massive sum, but it gets you in the game.

- Automate a process. Set up a CRM with at least some lightweight marketing automation. Craft some e-mails to go out every couple of weeks to introduce your company and have it trigger tasks for you to complete, like picking up the phone and calling.

- Try a different avenue. E-mailing is easy. So easy that everyone does it. Find ways to break through the communication noise. Send old-fashioned, handwritten notes or send something in a priority envelope. Nobody gets real mail anymore. It will get opened.

- Pick up the phone. I know, nobody uses them these days (guilty), but it's one of the easier ways to break through the noise *because* nobody uses them.

- Sprinkle time and money everywhere: search engines, social media, sponsorships, partnerships, referral programs, etc. Shake every tree and don't stop until nothing else falls or the effort to shake it is too great.

- Get creative. Do something that people remember. When you are memorable, people will mention it to others (pre-selling you internally). They'll also be more apt to take a second call if you manage to get the first.

BUILDING PIPELINE, REPEATABLE LEADS

If you were standing at the free-throw line, down by a point, would you rather have two shots to win the game or 100?

Two-thirds of the startups I've tried to help along the way fall in love with their early prospects and fail to build a pipeline. Whether it's identifying possible investors or prospective customers, the requirement is the same. You need as many chances to win as you can muster.

The constant need to focus only on the small handful of opportunities in which you're engaged leaves the pond dry once those fish have been caught. At that point, you start all over and it takes months to get to the same point. Having a sales funnel requires a constant flow of new prospects at the top in order to consistently close new business.

Two opposing psychological mentalities often get startups to focus on the seven or so opportunities that are right in front of them. One, the high of 'winning' a prospect and the low of being told 'no.'

Positive feedback is so rare at the early stages that our protection mechanism kicks in by focusing us on those first few people who express even the slightest bit of interest. It's validation, it feels great. Therefore, you pour all your energy into those select few.

But your attention isn't going to speed their timeline or dramatically increase your chances of winning the deal. Every deal has its own timeline. You can tweak at the margins to shorten it, but ultimately, it falls on your prospect.

At the opposite end of the spectrum are the countless 'nos' and non-responses. Because you're sifting through a sea of negative outcomes, it takes a lot more mental energy to focus on creating new leads at the top of the funnel than it does trying to close those at the bottom.

Hearing 'no thanks' is far less fun than pontificating about why your solution is amazing, especially to someone who has indicated they agree with you.

Their 'maybe' gets you in the game. It gives you an excuse to walk away from hearing no.

But. You can endure more than you think.

Getting to the point you have a repeatable sales model requires you to stop loving your current opportunities so much and to start loving the ones you don't yet have.

Consider These Actions:

- Set yourself a goal for the number of prospects at the top of the funnel, not just the dollars at the bottom. You need to feel a similar high gaining a prospect as you do when gaining a customer.

- Make ten new phone calls before following up on the prospect you've been in talks with for a while. The latter is easy, so treat it as dessert. Eat your vegetables first.

- Take a couple of hours each day to source new leads. It's never something that rises to the top of the list, but it's one of the more important things you can do.

MESSAGING SMALLER

What's the first thing everyone asks when they hear you've started a company?

"What do you do?"

Creating a pithy one-liner is more than trying to beg a second question. It means admitting there are things you don't do.

"It does x, y, *and* z."

If there were a way to monetize commas and 'ands' in startup descriptions, you'd have a unicorn business right there.

Because you don't know *exactly* what people want to buy, you try to throw everything into one big jumble. "We do it all!" But the odds are you're going up against larger, entrenched competitors and they *don't* do it all. Saying you do casts doubt rather than inspires confidence. It works against your own interests.

Your product may be better but creating a disconnect early leaves you climbing an even steeper hill to prove your value because people come in with an added dose of skepticism.

Describing your company is hard. We don't want to cut off a segment of the target audience by limiting what we say we do. This is especially true because we *know* we can solve any problem they have. Thus, we cram more solutions and more features into our descriptive overview in hopes of hitting upon the magic word our prospects are looking to hear.

It winds up looking something like,

> *Faux.io is an end-to-end platform for the insurance industry providing a dead simple way to put AI to work to proactively predict fraudulent claims, minimize payments to providers, and identify upsell opportunities.*

Perhaps a little exaggerated, but the first descriptive overview for nearly every startup up will have three commas, two 'ands,' the word 'easiest,' and a dusting of tech (not industry) buzzwords.

Winnowing your overview may reduce the size of the pool who opts in, but it means that you mean something to someone. That beats meaning nothing to a massive pool.

The one-liner is more critical than most realize. It is, after all, the first thing you say to a prospect. Spend days crafting it. See if you can meet the advertising industry's rule for billboard headlines of six words or less.

Commas confuse. 'Ands' dilute. Be clearer.

Consider These Actions:

- Message to sell like a predator. Predators don't take down the strongest, healthiest prey. They tend to eat the old, sick, or wounded. Tackle the problem at which the weakest competition is staking claim. As you eat them, you get stronger and can eat healthier prey.

- Focus on *what you solve*, not what your product does. The quickest way to bloat your overview is to start listing your features that tackle each step of a process.

- Leave out the benefits. Talk benefits after someone asks "why?".

- Say it in six words.

- Tell it to your mom. Use plain language to talk about the problem you're solving in a way she can understand. She should be able to explain it to her friends—because she will—and you never know who knows someone who may buy. Better yet, ask her to describe your company to you.

- Ask would-be prospects what they call the problem you're solving. Use their words if you hear them often. Different, clever turns of phrase just require you to educate more. Don't be clever.

FINDING TRIGGERING EVENTS

It's often said that selling is a numbers game. While there's truth to the idea of powering through a ton of 'nos,' I don't like the mentality because it makes it sound like there's no strategy involved to improve your success rate.

Selling is brawn *and* brains.

The constraint you have in the sales process is time. You can only fit so many phone calls, demos, follow-ups, and negotiations into a given day.

At the top of the funnel, the best way to maximize your time is to find great leads. That starts by proactively identifying the reasons people will talk with you. Those are the trigger moments that get your prospects to pay attention to your message. What is it about your customers that drive them? When does their world change so much that they know that the status quo won't cut it any longer?

Triggers have several characteristic. Specifically, they:

- happen consistently and frequently enough for you to maintain a healthy funnel;
- are large enough to force behavioral change; and
- are publicized (or, at least, somehow accessible to you)

Search engines have made the timing of triggering events easier to identify. Your prospects are raising their hand, asking you to come speak with them. The downside of easy is that anyone can take advantage of it. The more who seek to capitalize, the more expensive it gets. Thus, it's critical to look elsewhere in order to beat your competitors to the prospect and to find the less expensive trigger. Some examples are:

Personnel: Was someone recently hired? Look to trade journals who publish new executive hires, befriend headhunters in the target industry, and create online job alerts.

Regulatory: If a company is in an industry that mandates permitting, the government will publish a list of the most recently approved applicants.

Publicly Traded: If a company misses earnings a couple of quarters in a row, they may be more open to help or may disclose risks (albeit in non-descript boilerplate form) in their mandated filings.

The point is that there is data everywhere. Everything is a clue that leads you to understanding what your targets are facing. Use those clues to understand the triggers that open the door for you, then hit your numbers via interactions that are far more likely to progress down the funnel.

Consider These Actions:

- Have a process to automatically identify trigger events. This is a race against the clock. While selling software to distilleries, we religiously tracked the list of new licenses approved by the federal government. Some were still six to twelve-months away from needing us, but we had the conversation and often closed the deal well before they opened their doors. Our primary competitor asked me multiple times how we had already locked in a new distillery before he had even known they existed. It wasn't being clairvoyant, just religiously tracking publicly available information.

- Know your buyer's motivations. Get into the details about them. To whom do they report? Can you find when their boss leaves? What makes your buyer nervous? When does he or she have to make a change in order to find additional value in their process? For what are they held accountable? Map their professional lifecycle to get to the root of what will spring them into action.

- Use the trigger's perceived deadlines to force the timeline of a conversation. A deadline doesn't have to be an exact date, but deadlines spur action. Triggers help because they require change at some point (e.g. new hires' 100-day plans or next quarters' filings).

MASS-CUSTOMIZING THE SALES PITCH

We often think that there is one right answer to what our company does and the problems we solve.

And we're right.

The challenge, however, is that the single right message is different for everyone.

The push to 'find the right message' can be dangerous. It closes us off to alternative descriptions and approaches. The fact is that there are many reasons someone will buy from you. Your job is to understand the individual with whom you're talking and tailor your approach to meet their needs.

Imagine the initial call like a decision tree. The idea behind the decision tree pitch is that you have a mass customized presentation based on where they lead you as you ask questions. The end result is basically:

"What are you looking to solve?"
"We need to do [xyz] better."
"Perfect. That's why we got into this business. Our technology does that via [abc] which improves [xyz] by 37%."

While selling HR software, we had modules that helped hiring, learning and development, engagement, and team dynamics. Telling someone that it helped in all those areas wasn't helpful. For one, no other software had introduced that model before. Second, few people had a job that spanned the breadth of those challenges.

We learned, via losing deals, that we couldn't lay it all out there and assume people would pay attention to the relevant pieces. We had to ask the right questions (note: these are a step well beyond the standard qualifying questions).

Our presentation was based on what they wanted to solve, how they're currently solving it, what they'd tried previously, and why those solutions didn't work.

With each question, we whittled the message, and conversely the demo, down to the piece that worked.

It won't win 100% of the prospects, but it will increase your win rate.

A couple of extra percent here and there add up to an additional month's worth of revenue, for the same cost, before too long.

Consider These Actions:

- Focus on the status quo or your prospect's company's failed prior attempts to address the challenge. Few prospects can envision the right solution to their challenge, but they can absolutely tell you why past attempts failed. Show that you're not that.

- Judge the personality. How people respond to your questions tells you more than just the answer. It tells you how they like to be spoken to as well. If they're quick and to the point in their responses, don't provide long-winded answers or cute anecdotes. Get to the point. If they're warm and open, explore your commonalities and build rapport.

- If you present with a deck, create a dozen of them so you can always lead with the version whose first slide miraculously says you solve the challenge they just described. It sounds like a lot of work, but it's just retooling the same deck to have different starting points and the likely objections the new starting point brings.

FIRING BAD PROSPECTS

It's hard to look at the big fish and say, "Not for me."

Revenue is nice, but not every customer is worth acquiring.

Some will reclaim your margin through your team's time. Some by producing constant threats about leaving if their feature isn't produced. And some will just demoralize the team with a constant drip of negativity and complaining.

Acknowledging the soft costs of a new customer will help you draw a line that you won't let prospects cross. Arming your sales team with these lines gives them the permission to say 'no.' And with the permission to say 'no' they can do a better job of protecting the other teams.

Sometimes it's obvious that a prospect will make your life miserable if they start paying you because they're making your life miserable when they *aren't* paying you.

It matters because your team is only as productive as they choose to be. When they enjoy the customers (even in the midst of hearing about bugs) it's easier for them to stay a few extra minutes to answer one more question.

But when customers are treating them poorly and you sit idly by because the revenue matters more, they become miserable. It takes them a bit longer to reply to support tickets, the answers are a hair less thorough, and at 5:01 p.m. the office is deserted.

Even more costly than misery, is distraction.

Often, that distraction often comes from large prospects. Your solution seems to be working well for others in the space, so the Fortune100 calls you up. They like your solution, but just need this one additional thing.

You're flattered and immediately seduced.

But 'no' has to be an arrow in your quiver.

Larger companies aren't used to hearing 'no.' Especially from startups. So, they offer to pay for development. It becomes easy to allow them to drive the product roadmap in a way that isn't beneficial for your broader customer base.

Before long you've created custom software at a tiny fraction of the price. Now you're left supporting this new feature with the same headcount and yet it still demands 'just one more tweak.'

While justifying the updated product roadmap as 'letting the customers drive the road map' or through a belief that the large customer's logo attracts new customers, it's sucking you dry.

Keeping the lights on is a constant battle. While revenue is critical, it's not all created equally. Even if you don't turn the bad prospects away before they become customers, recognize what a bad customer looks like and at least question whether you'd be better off without them or whether you need to charge a hefty annual maintenance fee to support them.

Consider These Actions:

- Know the limit. At what point do you say 'no'? Give thought to unacceptable behaviors and what requests get the firmly polite 'no.' Sometimes just having a well-reasoned rationale will get prospects to look at you differently.

- Seek another point of contact. Sometimes it's not the company, but the person. Before completely ditching the revenue opportunity, find another point of contact. They may have a different perspective on the minimum needs.

- Recommend your competitors. Though you help them generate a few extra dollars, recommending needy prospects to your competitors will chip away at their ability to keep up with you because the new customer(s) will drain their time, resources, and focus. Weaken your competition by helping them 'win' business.

- If they're already a customer, experiment with them. Think you can charge more? Start with the customers who you wanted to fire anyway.

DE-RISKING YOUR SOLUTION

If you're selling in the B2B world, you'll find others aren't like you.

Where you chase exponential value through risk, many corporate buyers seek stability and safety. Where you are at the top of the org chart, the corporate buyer has a boss evaluating them on a narrow slice of the business. Your product isn't the reason they will get promoted or see a large bonus.

Selling your product can often be as much about selling safety as it is about selling something 'game-changing.' Not everyone is comfortable buying 'game-changing.'

Crafting your unique selling proposition must bear all this in mind. It's not a matter of being the 'unique-est,' but a matter of nailing the intersection of the buyer's need and their risk tolerance.

A point of differentiation can be scary to those who are risk averse. Odds are that they'd rather continue buying from those whom they've always bought. Or if they're looking to change, they may be seeking someone who satisfies the needs in a similar, familiar manner with the slight bonus of making things a little easier, being a little more accurate, or finding someone who can absorb blame if things go wrong.

Entrepreneurs who cross over into sales find this path a bumpy one. Very few people have an entrepreneur's risk tolerance.

A startup in the traffic management space had a wonderful product that could provide traffic counts to transportation officials within the day instead of the six-month process currently in place.

The product was 99-percent quicker and a tick more accurate.

Sales stemmed from the latter. People would get fired for being wrong, but not for being slow.

The cost of screwing up far outweighed the gains of being fast.

Accuracy was safety. Speed seemed risky. Speed sounded like errors. And bad data quickly was more dangerous than bad data that took time because it was different.

Sometimes a uniquely unique selling proposition is wholly legitimate and exactly what an accelerator or investor tells you to chase. Sometimes those same propositions can add risk to your sales cycle and reduce your win rate. Knowing your buyer will allow you to know which case is right for you.

Consider These Actions:

- Profile your buyer. This is obvious, but rarely probed deeply enough. Knowing your buyers isn't just understanding their problems, but understanding their psyche, their power (or lack thereof), who evaluates them and what that individual cares about, and their risk tolerance. Your strength must complement them.

- Have someone challenge your assumptions. It's hard to see both sides yourself, so grab someone who is naturally contrarian (and preferably empathetic to your customer). Present your advantages to them and ask them to tell you why they aren't actually advantages.

- Experiment. Barring a deep psychological profile of your buyer, try different types of messaging. Flip the script so you lead with alternative types of differentiation points. Gauge reactions, objections, and win rates throughout to see how they differ.

- When in doubt, ask. Ask them what they want from their jobs and what they need to do in order to reach that. If you can help, you've landed on the 'advance to the next stage of the sales funnel' space.

SELLING A STORY

There are a million and one sales books out there and every seven years or so there's a new sales process that's en vogue.

I can't tell you whether today's popular sales approach is right for you, but selling isn't just about challenging, spinning, or 'snap'ping your prospect. It's about understanding who they are, what they need, and how you can help.

It starts by asking, listening, and confirming. Then it's reinforced by the stories you share that illustrate how well you understand their situation.

Stories, not facts and figures, sell. Story telling is the most critical piece that is too often overlooked. We tend to pitch rationally. But that's not how people buy.

Even enterprise buyers are people first. They want to be entertained and painted a picture of what the future looks like. It's not that much different than getting someone to imagine themselves in a new SUV climbing the mountain to a remote hiking spot. Will they ever take the truck off-road? Not likely. But they like to imagine they are the type who lives carefree on that mountaintop.

Your story doesn't have to be fanciful like the SUV, but it has to be colorful enough so that your prospect imagines a better work situation when they're using your product.

There is a time and place for logic. But it rarely sets the hook. Emotion keeps the conversation going long enough to make logic powerful.

Logic and calculations are useful when assuring the prospect they're making the right choice. Nobody likes to be hoodwinked, so the defenses will go up toward the end. Appealing to their logical selves at this point pacifies the nagging feeling that they rushed to judgement.

Emotion sells, logic justifies.

Consider These Actions:
- Take the days or weeks to craft the heroic stories to suit all types of motivations. You want a library of stories that you can seamlessly tell upon learning why the prospect is taking the time to speak with you. When crafting your stories, consider:

Being Lois, Not Superman

It may be counterintuitive but the stories you tell are not about you or your product. They are about that customer who was in the same predicament as your current prospect. In your story, that customer became a hero. That customer was Superman. You are Lois Lane telling the story.

Addressing Objections Early and Emotions Throughout

Before you can get to triggering emotions, you have to get the objections out of the way. You know what they are likely to be, so hit them head on.

Without addressing them, your prospect will be evaluating your demo waiting to see if it addresses the objection in their head. It's natural to be skeptical when a person is on the receiving end of a sales demo. They're protecting themselves from being taken advantage of by thinking through the ways and reasons why what you say won't work. Take away the objections early so they can focus on what you're actually saying.

Letting Your Prospects be Smart

Leaving questions open gives your prospect the chance to be smart. They need to ask the hard questions in order to feel confident that they've done their due diligence. Stop early and often to ask what they're thinking, whether they see any reasons it wouldn't work for them, or to ask a leading question about an objection that usually arises. You likely know the questions but there are no bonus points granted for answering them prior to being asked.

Being Succinct

When you've been enmeshed in your area of expertise without having a ton of sales success, you're desperate to prove you know what you're talking about. The tendency will be to over-explain, to lead them on your learning journey so they are as knowledgeable as you and that they trust your intellect.

Stop. Tell them what they need to know and leave space for them to dig into the areas in which they want to know more. They'll decide if they want to test you.

It used to be said that if you asked my grandfather the time, you'd hear how a watch worked. Busy people just want the time.

SELLING EMOTION

You've built an ROI calculator, haven't you?

Winning new customers is a function of how compelling the post-sale story is that you create. Why your customer can easily become the 'after' photo in the side by side. Odds are, that's not the story you're telling.

Entrepreneurs tend to think big picture and because you run your own company, you are also likely to dwell upon the bottom line. Spending a dollar to save five is compelling to you.

So, you build ROI calculators and carefully construct the rationale for how beneficial your product is to the customer's own bottom line. You're selling pure, irrefutable logic.

Thus, you spend your time with the customer, walking them through it, when it'd be better spent listening to the pain they have. Pain stirs emotion.

Rarely is their problem that they need to recoup their investment on your product. They're looking to clear the decks of tedious, error-prone work, or to simply make their own life easier. Something has become too annoying to ignore.

People buy on that emotion. ROI is just something they can use to sell internally to get approval. Important to know, but only relevant after your buyer has bought in.

Why most people don't see your ROI:

- Outside of Corporate Development and Business Operations groups, very few people are ever rewarded for their investment decisions. Purchasing your product may save your team all sorts of time but from the bean counters' perspective, you are still just an added cost.
- Everyone assumes they are different. If you're selling across industries people won't believe the ROI calculations work for their specific industry. If you're selling within a single industry, everyone believes their company is uniquely dysfunctional. "The ROI calculator couldn't possibly hold for us," goes the thinking.

- Opportunity costs are never calculated for employees. If things become more efficient, they may 'see' the return by laying someone off, but that's not likely. The assumption is that the time you save isn't filled with revenue-generating activities. Often because they aren't, but also because the value of the new actions taken is often invisible.

Consider These Actions:

- Focus on the prospect's challenges. Remind them of the pain and show how your product is the ointment that can land them in the 'after' photo. Everything from your website to your pitch to your follow-through should highlight how you address the issues that cause pain.

- Have your existing customers 'sell' your product back to you. Ask them how you can better sell your product and listen to the value points they mention. Get them to talk about *how* their job has changed. Listen for the change in emotions, not the change in actions.

- Remember it's not about you. Create the before and after picture. How does your buyer become a hero? You are selling the ability to be Superman. On your best days you get to be Lois Lane reporting out your customer's heroism. Usually, you're just the dry cleaner who pressed the suit.

BEATING STATUS QUO

Whether a prospect is looking to do something for the first time or to replace something they already have, there is a process in place that addresses what your solution does. If there truly is no process that exists, they've simply made the conscious choice that the challenge isn't yet worth solving.

No matter what they teach in school, what your investors tell you, or what you are told by your prospects, your competition isn't your biggest competitor.

Status quo is.

The status quo is a beast to unseat. Costs and pains are viewed as constants. People default to the mentality that that's the way it is, that's the way it's always been, and that's what the forecast calls for.

The status quo is known.

Buying requires changing behavior. And behavior change is hard.

You must paint a picture of what the world should look like. That means getting your prospect to imagine themselves living in that world and addressing the concerns that arise in their imagination.

There is a reason that get-rich-quick schemes and exercise-free weight-loss programs will never go away. Everyone wants the outcome without the effort. That's what you're selling.

If you can extract so much value out of your product that it makes people forget about the effort they applied, then you will win.

Nobody cares about you or your product. They care about their own time, the professional challenges they face, and how to fulfill their personal goals. Your product is a means to an end, not *the* end.

Attacking the status quo requires every team to play a part. It starts by describing the post-change world and showing how your product leads to that desired outcome (marketing and sales). Then you need someone there to hold them accountable and ensure they aren't cheating by reverting back to their old methods (account management).

Finally, you need the product itself to display the progress made to keep the dopamine dripping to ensure the pleasure from using the product is greater than the pain of doing what they had been doing (product team).

Changing behavior requires a team of supporters.

Consider These Actions:

- Know why. Some industries are still using MS-DOS. Clearly, it's not *not* working or else they'd have changed decades ago. The longer a solution has been in place, the harder it is to evolve. It's the devil they know. While doing your customer discovery, focus not just on validating pain points, but on why they haven't taken action.

- Know your buyer. How is the end-user evaluated in their job? What are the expectations for accomplishing the part of the job around which you want to help? New is risk. New could increase expectations placed upon them. New could expose something they should have been doing but haven't. You can't just assume that people want to solve the problem you see. For some people, change is a bug, not a feature.

- Subtract from people's jobs, don't add. Nobody needs one more thing to do. The problem you solve may fall directly in someone's purview, but if their bosses aren't paying attention to it then it's not part of their job. You'll never convince someone to buy if doing so will increase their workload or add something for which the buyer will be newly accountable.

ADDRESSING DISREPUTABLE COMPETITION

Not every competitor will play fair.

If you're doing a halfway decent job, there will be someone out there who will copy your product, tell lies about your shortcomings, and generally spread misinformation about your company. It's inevitable.

You will be angry. You'll want revenge. You'll want to bury them.

It's also a no-win trap. Time is your most precious resource. The more you spend focused on playing your competitor's game, the less you can focus on re-writing the rules of the game. The more money you spend on lawyers, the less time you have before you have to raise the next round of funding (or hiring more time, if you're bootstrapping).

You are being targeted for a reason. You've done well and proven that you're a real threat in the marketplace. Keep your attention focused on what's gotten you there and make the competition continue chasing you.

Matching their shameless inaccuracies isn't the way to go either. That is a race to the bottom. Instead, arm your prospects with the questions they should ask your competitor. These questions will highlight your relative strengths and shine the light on the competitor's weaknesses. Identify the things the competitor does well and mention those. Give your prospects the information they need to make the right choice.

Consider your judo options.

At one point our primary competitor bought a misspelling of our company's name (transposing two letters that seemed to get transposed all the time...even for us internally. In fact, we only discovered it because an employee mistyped the URL on her own browser). The competitor redirected the URL to his own site. Everyone was appalled by his lack of professionalism and it was the topic of conversation all morning.

I was furious. It was slimy. I immediately bought three misspellings of his company's name and before I could set the URLs up to forward to our own domain, the employee who discovered the issue came into my office and said we shouldn't act like him and that we were the leaders in the market because we held ourselves to a higher standard.

She was 100% right and called me out for acting out of anger. It was a one of the best possible teaching moments for me. I was being shown how to model the behavior to which they wanted to be held accountable.

Instead, I directed all the URLs to our competitor's site and gave him a call.

I told him how we thought his actions were unprofessional and that we didn't want to compete against him like that but that we also weren't going to let bad behavior go unchecked. I told him we'd bought three misspellings of his company's name to his one, but that we'd directed them back to his proper website.

The implication was clear. We'll outspend you on this nonsense and 'win' this fight, but we don't want to go down that path. He understood and agreed to reroute the original URL and let them expire the following year so we could each reclaim our own.

Months later, a new company entered the market with a beautiful user interface. A little too beautiful. It was the same one that we'd been working on for the prior year. It was so similar, in fact, that the images in his product were pixelated because they were lifted directly from our demonstration videos.

Having learned from the prior experience, I called the owner of the company and got a different response; a dramatically less professional 'no thank you.'

So, we took the side-by-side comparisons we'd captured and made that a part of our sales process. We were selling to distillers and brewers, a group of craftspeople who generally believed in integrity and hard work. But they were also a very price-sensitive group and inevitably, we'd be asked about this new low-cost competitor.

Our reaction was scripted to remain dispassionate and professional. We acknowledged the huge cost savings they provided, but reminded our prospect that the reason they were buying was because they needed someone they could trust to navigate the complexities of the federal regulations. We were (professionally) saying that they were deciding between partnering with the one who knows *why* the math works or the one who copies the homework of the one who understands.

Typically, it's not worth the energy and capital expended to duke these things out. If someone is copying you or trying to blindside you then it's an admission of inferiority.

They will always be playing catch up. Just keep going. Stay focused and make it make you better.

In the end, you want to be the person you want your employees to be. They are always watching and what you do will be modeled later. People want to be proud of their employer's actions and know that they won't have to be someone they don't like in order to be successful at your company. How you proceed is how others will proceed when they're faced with a similar decision down the line.

Consider These Actions:

- Sell the slight. Build the slime into your sales process. Don't allow your salespeople to talk down about your competition, but give them the ability to arm your prospects with the questions to ask the competition when they get a demo from them. Always encourage them to seek out that demo, but request they talk to you last.

- Use it to motivate. Nobody likes to see their work ripped off. Use it to your advantage to refocus the team's efforts on the things that will let you run further in front of the competition.

- Use it to waste competitor's time. Use an hour or two of your lawyer's time to send the cease and desist letter, as well as a couple of follow-on demand letters. Even without any intention to do anything about it, you can still get them spun up to think about the fight. Distraction loses.

SELLING TO THE INCOME STATEMENT

A buck is a buck, except when it's not.

It stands to reason that earning an extra dollar is the same as saving a dollar, which is why new companies will often calculate ROI for their customers pulling from both sides. But those dollars aren't equal.

When you sell revenue there is a bright-line connection to your product.

It's the first line of the income statement. There is nothing that will interfere with the value you're bringing. None of the other line items can eat into the contribution you made. You can show, month over month, the value you brought.

Conversely, selling cost savings (lower on the income statement), your value isn't recognized until you hit the very last line. By then, dozens of other line items have been added and subtracted. The value you brought is opaque and easily attributable to something else.

Worse, the money you saved them will just paper over another department going over budget. That's completely out of your control. It's the tragedy of the commons.

Barring turnaround situations, most department leaders get evaluated more favorably for their ability to drive growth rather than save a buck.

Cost savings are invisible. Selling cost savings is like proving a counterfactual. It can be done, but you need your audience to take a leap of faith with you.

At RoundPegg, we were able to improve hiring outcomes by identifying those who would perform better and stay longer.

The cost of turnover is incredibly high (between 50% and 400% of someone's annual salary).

Building an ROI calculator was a no-brainer. If we saved a company two bad hires, we paid for ourselves. The real numbers were staggering. Given our pricing, a 50-100x return on the investment wasn't just possible, but probable.

Not only was the ROI too great (we had to lop a zero off the ROI calculator to make it believable), but the entire ROI was based on cost savings.

Sales remained sluggish and the ROI calculator was eventually discarded.

We didn't recognize it at the time, but when we focused on sales teams, ears perked up.

By showing the increase in the percentage of quota met by the sales reps that our software had identified as better fits, we were able to highlight our value via new revenue generated.

We weren't smart enough to see it then and attack it religiously, but selling revenue completely changed our sales conversations.

Consider These Actions:

- Find the revenue use case. Saving time and money is valuable, but if there is a revenue-producing use case, it can help you swim downstream.

- Get creative. Reducing customer churn is another way to 'sell revenue,' particularly in a SaaS business. Similarly, opening up time for those who produce revenue will generate more revenue. There's more than one way to sell into revenue. How you do it depends on the value you bring and the group who uses your product.

- Stop calculating the squishy. If you sell efficiency (e.g. streamlining workflow, time savings), don't quantify it. Sell the emotion. Knowing there's a better way is frustrating. There's anguish. People in that situation buy with their heart, not their brain.

RESPONDING TO THE PRICE QUESTION

"How much is it?"

Too often we feel a need to rationalize our price. That it needs to be justified in a way that gets the prospect to accept it. This leads to a response that begins with, "well, we have a couple of different options, but all of them include…"

Just. Say. The. Price.

As soon as you start to justify, your prospect gets frustrated because you're not answering their question and they hear your own doubt in your pricing model. When you start justifying it before they object, it says, "our product isn't worth it" or "negotiate me down."

The strongest response to "how much is it?" is simply telling them how much it costs and then to stop talking.

If you've already explained a lot of the benefits, then you can confidently stop talking. Even if you haven't, it's worthwhile to zip it. By not immediately reiterating your benefits, you're implicitly saying, "This is how much it costs and it's worth it."

That's not to say you won't get an objection, a scoff, or an attempt to belittle the value (it's a poor negotiator's first tactic). But giving your prospect the space to say the next line will give you the most valuable information possible; how likely they are to buy and what value they place on your product.

If they indicate the price is too high, *then* you can go into your typical explanation of how you price, what discounts are available, and the value points you provide, or flip the script to ask again about their challenges. If they start talking about the budget they may have to cut to implement it, you know they see the value. Their reply gives you your next move. Listen carefully.

Consider These Actions:
- Keep your pricing sheet in front of you. Your prospect is looking for a number. Even when you know your prices cold, you don't want to pause. Having the price list with you allows you to advance with more confidence.

- Practice saying it. It sounds hokey but film yourself giving your pitch and saying the price. The more it comes out of your mouth the more believable it becomes to you.

- Pay attention to how annoying it is when you ask a vendor for the price and don't get it immediately. Same goes for the answer to any question. You'll want to get right to the point with your prospects. Not being the 'bad sales guy' gives you more confidence in how you're performing.

INCREASING VELOCITY - IT'S NOT YOUR PRICE

Too often when a deal drags, the founder tasked with sales will default to cutting the price. It's natural. The price feels totally made up, so you assume you've made up the wrong one. Further, we equate how much that revenue means to our little company with how much it costs our prospect's company. The two aren't remotely close to equal.

Price is rarely the last hurdle.

We believe our price is too high until we understand the true value of the product we've built. Not only have few people validated it for us (by giving us money), we place no value on our time and getting *any* revenue is better than getting none.

There are countless reasons why someone hasn't signed after indicating their interest. They got busy with another project. A team member just quit. They have a sick parent. They are working on convincing someone it's required but don't want to admit *to you* that they aren't the ultimate decision maker.

The assumptions you make cost you money on the current deal—and every one that follows.

Instead, be forthright and ask, "Something is holding you back from working with us, what is it? What can I do to help?"

You may not get the truth, but you won't be lighting dollars on fire in hopes that the pricing sideshow entertains them enough to sign. It's not just the cost of the lost revenue you could have obtained with this prospect but the steady devaluing of your product when the next prospect gets hung up. Add up enough of these and you convince yourself you need to cut pricing across the board. That puts more pressure on closing larger numbers of prospects.

We also tend to default to price because we subconsciously draw a parallel between enterprise sales dollars and our company's budget. There is none. Prospects who are used to cutting deals are used to seeing six and seven figures. That may be well above your company's monthly payroll and is well beyond what your checking account has ever seen, but it shouldn't scare you from trying to charge that amount.

I once had a prospect tell me that their wine budget was bigger than what we were asking to charge. That was almost embarrassing. Unless this is the first time someone is dealing with a real contract for the company, the money is often a rounding error in the grand scheme of things. Don't be afraid to get your share of the value you bring.

For many of your prospects, this is Monopoly™ money. It's so far out of the realm of what they spend in their real lives that it's just a number.

So, don't give on price until they ask.

Consider These Actions:

- Create pressure via the prospect's own timelines. Artificial deadlines are simply transparent bluffs. Understanding the internal workings of your prospect's role will help you find a critical point around which you can base a deadline.

- Be forthright. Ask what's holding up the deal. Ask them if their budget has a hole about the size of what you're asking. They may not tell you the full truth, but you'll put them in a position where they can. If nothing else, it will start a dialogue around the price at which they can sign quickly.

- Walk away. Sometimes people just can't say no. They don't want to hurt your feelings, so they waste their time and yours instead.

INCREASING VELOCITY, NO > MAYBE

There is a real opportunity cost to chasing 'maybe.'

Time is the currency of sales. The more quickly you can move a prospect from one stage to the next, the more you free up a space to backfill with another prospect. Greater funnel velocity affords you more chances to close a sale.

The worst prospect is the one who won't tell you no. People inadvertently (and intentionally) lead on salespeople all the time.

They want to feel important. They want to learn what competitors are doing. They want leverage with which to renegotiate with their current vendor.

Or it could be as simple as they like you and don't want to make you feel bad.

Whatever the reason, it's just as critical for you to push for a no as it is for a yes. It doesn't feel right in the moment because you're closing a door but chasing them down to set up the next meeting or providing additional research costs you time that could be better spent on prospects who are more likely to purchase.

While I don't believe sales is a numbers game because you can do a lot to affect your numbers, I do believe it's a velocity game. Time kills all deals and the better you can manage your time and push prospects through your process, the more effective you will be.

Maybe is the *absolute* worst.

There's a reason the deal hasn't closed and either they don't know, or they aren't telling you. In your mind, there is a magic phrase you can say, and you just need a few more guesses. But you may as well be trying to guess the number they're thinking. That's a game with terrible odds.

A salesperson only has so many actions they can take in a day. While there's always wasted time checking social media or making tea, you want to try to eliminate as many unforced errors as possible. One of the best ways to do that is to be more ruthless about killing deals.

Consider These Actions:

- Ask for a no. Many prospects become 'maybes' because they don't want to feel badly about themselves by making you feel bad. Give them the 'no' to give back to you. "Tell me if I'm wrong, but it seems like you're not in a position to buy our solution. My feelings won't be hurt if that's the case, but you're busy and I don't want you to feel like you have to dodge me when I try to get in touch." Basically, "stop wasting my time..." politely. If you've misread the situation and they are still likely to sign, they'll tell you and give you a solid timeframe. "No, no, I'm still interested, but I just can't do anything until our budgets are unfrozen next quarter."

- Keep clean data. Know the true number of days someone has been in the funnel. There must be a very clear triggering event that puts them on the board. If the trigger for a start date is fuzzy then your data is worthless. When you get enough velocity, you can see the (typically) normal distribution of the time to close. When someone starts leaking beyond a standard deviation past the median, it's time to move them to 'no.'

- Follow a process. Have a plan for the cadence of the outreach. Stretch the plan to cover 75% of when all sales close. After that, make the sales rep prove that someone should stay in the funnel. They need to sell you on why the prospect is relevant.

GETTING BETAS TO PAY

In the rush to hear 'yes,' the free beta offer is always on the tip of your tongue. The argument is that you need to get some traction, hear feedback on the product, and create testimonials.

The hardest part of creating a company is not building something that contains value but whether you can sell that value for more than it costs to create.

That requires getting feedback on the sales side as well as the product side.

Charging even a single dollar changes the mindset. It suddenly presents you with rejection. But when you're successful it proves that there's a market. It doesn't prove you have a business, but it does prove the problem exists and that people will pay *something* to make it go away.

Noted behavioral economist Dr. Dan Ariely sought to test the effects of free by offering chocolates to his students.

The logical assumption was that given the choice of a vastly superior product at a reasonable price (i.e. benefits minus cost was high) versus an inferior product that had very little excess benefit (i.e. benefits minus cost was lower) that the former should win out every time.

Naturally, that's not how things turned out.

Offering "One Chocolate Per Student" to MIT students, the researchers stocked lower value Hershey's Kisses and higher value Lindt chocolate truffles. When the costs were a penny and a quarter, respectively, people overwhelmingly chose the truffle for a quarter.

But when the experiment was repeated after lowering the price one penny each (i.e. free Hershey's Kiss vs. $0.24 truffle), things changed. The mental benefit less cost calculation should have produced the same results, but nearly everyone chose the free Hershey's Kiss.

When things are free nobody accounts for the non-financial costs. Think of the number of people who stand in line for free Ben & Jerry's ice cream every year. The lines are down the block. People are willing to wait a half hour to get something worth a couple of dollars. It's a terrible return on their investment (assuming they're employed), but the pain of spending doesn't exist when a product is free.

It's the pain of incurring a cost that you and your sales process need to solve. The challenge is rarely what feature to build, but rather, what are people willing to pay to solve their problem.

Consider These Actions:

- Seriously, just charge *something. Anything.* While Dr. Ariely's implications show that even charging a buck is enough to change the behavior and make overcoming the 'no' a real thing for your sales process, charge enough that it feels like something worthwhile internally.

- Seek out the 'no.' If everyone is saying 'yes' to your 'no' or low price, raise it. You don't just want to hear 'no,' you need it. Without objections you won't know how to overcome them later.

- Give betas a blank check. Learn a little something about pricing while you're at it. Tell the beta prospect that they can name their price. The only rule is they have to pay *something.* You may find they're willing to pay a lot more than you think. If nothing else, it's a great marketing approach to make a name for your small company.

- If you have free betas in the fold already, read *Converting Free Betas.*

CREATING URGENCY

You don't buy a winter coat in the summer. If you do, it's because time is running out on a deal you can't possibly refuse. All buying requires a sense of urgency.

That urgency is best solved by addressing a pain that is so great people just want it to stop. That's rarely the case, however, because most products are incremental improvements that still require effort to implement.

There is one other way to create urgency. Use your prospects internal timelines in your favor.

There is a reason your prospect reached out or took your call on the day she did. We're usually so giddy that someone called us back that we fail to ask, 'why now?'. But it's knowing the 'why now' that can lead to a faster close. (It also helps identify the triggering events to source other prospects.)

Perhaps there was an internal reorganization and your prospect is new to her role. Or she's opening a new facility and needs to have the infrastructure in place. Or she has a new product launching soon.

All of those reasons have a timeline behind them. Something happens on a given date and there's an expectation behind it. Even the seemingly innocuous 'new to the role' rationale has the company's Quarterly Business Review (QBR) meeting or performance review looming. If your product can be a bullet point in the positive column for either, that's meaningful.

Once you understand the reason and the timing, you can work backward to give them a deadline by which they must sign. Along the way, you're setting expectations for the onboarding timeline and the time you need. You reframe their thinking by showing that it's using your product, not just signing the deal, that must meet their timeline. That requires the salesperson broaden the aperture and think into the job-description box of the account managers. That's always a positive.

Consider These Actions:
- Ask. You can't understand what's going to drive your prospect to put pen to paper unless you understand what deadlines and goals she faces.

- Remind. Each time you speak with your prospect, (gently) remind them of their deadline.
- Understand who else needs to approve. Knowing who else needs to say 'yes' gives you more chances to find legitimate deadlines around which to base a signing. While group decision-making processes are rife with downsides, one silver lining is more opportunities to create urgency.

CLOSING MORE - TIME KILLS ALL DEALS

Every sale is made up of a handful to hundreds of interactions. Each of those interactions takes time. And it's time—not what you say or how you've priced—that is the biggest killer of your deals.

From the second a lead is generated, the clock starts. If somebody has provided their information on your website, they've given you permission to speak with them (so long as you call them while they're still thinking about you). As soon as they press submit, they've mentally checked the box of looking for the answer to their problem and are moving onto the next task, checking their social media feed, or socializing with a colleague.

Every step of the process is exactly like this. If you miss the window to get back to them, it may take a week or two to establish that next interaction.

There are too many variables outside your control that you can't let your unavailability be one. It's such a simple one to eliminate and the one that is wholly in your control.

Every step of the process requires speed.

If someone is thinking about you (or experiencing the pain your product will solve), you need to call them. You have a tiny window to catch your prospect when they're still open to your message. As soon as they go back to their day, you free fall down the list of priorities. Talk to them when you're their priority rather than getting back to them when it's convenient for you.

Do that and you'll be far more likely to advance to the next stage of the deal. Do it enough times and you'll see the win percentage increase.

Consider These Actions:

- Always, always, always follow up with a lead within five minutes. If you can't call them right back, have someone else do it. It doesn't matter if the one who is free to call doesn't handle that territory. If you lose the scent, it's nobody's lead.

- Track the time it takes to respond to leads, to close a deal, and the time in between each step of the process. You treasure what you measure. Treasure speed.

- Put a process in place to react when your prospect is thinking about you. With so many tech tools in place to track who is doing what with your e-mails or on your website, you need a proactive way to use them to your advantage. See someone just opened your e-mail? Pick up the phone and call them that second.

NAVIGATING THE INTERNAL CHAMPION

The internal champion is the ultimate sales bank shot.

The idea of an internal champion selling your product internally is a tall order. They don't have experience selling, they don't know your product as well as you, and they tend have more to lose than gain by selling you.

Your champion should be your guide rather than an extension of your sales team. Earn their trust to allow you to represent them in the process. They are more valuable identifying the doubters, objections, and biases you'll face rather than staring those forces down themselves.

You need your champion to help you sell internally, not to do it themselves.

To close the deal, you'll need to guide those internal discussions yourself. You never know how much juice your champion has. Their lack of expertise, social capital, or influence can kill a deal.

Before you can sell your product, you sometimes have to sell your ability to cast your champion in a warm glow, so they allow you to represent them to others.

For example, when selling into Human Resources, we often created one-sheets for the HR champion to use to help sell the need to the CFO. It was a detailed cost/benefit analysis that pulled the curtain back on the true costs of a poor hire and painted the picture of what the world looked like after buying our product.

It was gorgeous and airtight. But it never worked. Not once.

Two years later I was spending time with a Gartner analyst who casually dropped a bombshell on me. "You know, we surveyed HR leaders in the EU and only 6% said they were comfortable with quantitative analyses."

The internal sales collateral wasn't working because it was never being presented. Our champion was afraid. Presenting our analysis would have exposed their discomfort with backing up the analysis. One question and they'd have been sunk. They didn't want to put themselves in that position.

When we started showing them what we'd like to talk to their CFO about, the objections we thought we'd hear, and how we'd respond, we gave them confidence that we would make them look good. Their mental calculation of the risk we posed representing them was reduced, so they'd occasionally facilitate the meeting. It didn't make sales any easier, but we weren't hanging around, hoping that the prospect who talked a big game fell out the bottom of the funnel.

Forget the champion. Find a Sherpa.

Consider These Actions:

- Walk the halls. Even if just metaphorically, push to be in each of the various meetings. Ultimately, you want to be the one to address concerns head-on because you've heard the concerns before and know the foil for each.

- Talk through the players. Ask your champion who is involved and specifically, who are the skeptics and why, what politics are involved, and what each of the players is looking to prove.

- Shoot a video. Create a custom 90-second video specifically for the skeptic. Speak to their issues, if you know them, but above all else, convey your desire to serve. (Receiving a tailored message – "Hi Bob from Accounting…" is nothing if not flattering.)

- Write up an objection list. *Show* your champion you're prepared so they trust you to represent them well.

NEGOTIATING THE DEAL

There is nearly always a deal to be had.

If you go into a negotiation with that mentality, you'll be far more likely to widen the aperture of possibilities that gets everyone what they need.

Lead off.

The negotiation points and metrics tend to take the form of whomever lays out the details first. You're not just anchoring price, but anchoring the salient points that are up for discussion in the partnership. For most people, it's far easier to tweak something that exists than it is to draw something up from scratch.

Putting the first offer out there puts you in control. Negotiations are a confidence game. Leading off tells the other side you possess it. Getting it, however, is a function of preparation. Specifically:

Know the economic boundaries.
Negotiation experts will tell you that the key is knowing the point at which you walk away, the cost of your prospect's alternative solution, and the value they get from your solution. If you know those three points, you see the entire playing field.

It sounds so easy, but you never have perfect information on any of these points. Your preparation beforehand can lead you to estimates that you'll want to confirm as you progress. For example, if you think it'll cost them ten million dollars and one year to build your product, get details on their capabilities and focus. What opportunities are they chasing? Do they have unutilized headcount to staff the project (e.g. if dozens of jobs are posted, the prospect is likely already spread thin)? How much cash they have on hand?

Knowing your value.
That ROI calculator you have does serve a purpose. This is where it's worth trotting out. The value it shows may be outrageous, but it's a good anchor. Sharing the information with your prospect and asking for their thoughts can provide information about what they value, in addition to setting the ceiling.

Know your prospect's alternatives.
The alternatives they have vary from the status quo to your competitors to building something in-house. Each come with a cost; not the least of which is time. When formulating the value you bring, it must be in the context of the alternatives. Figuring out those fuzzy lines will give you a sense of their desired path and what they can afford.

Know your costs
You can't negotiate a deal that works for you if you don't know what doesn't work. A deal that doesn't work is one that costs you money. Those are deals where you'd be better off simply not being in business.

When you're dealing with unknowns, you have to make your best guesses. The more math you put behind it the closer you're likely to be.

The marginal cost to service a new customer is the absolute bare minimum you can charge. Taking a 60-100% margin above that should be closer to the goal. The early days make marginal costs difficult to calculate. The effort to model out the time required to service the deal will give you a better starting point upon which to have confidence.

The more effort you put into triangulating the points above, the more confident you'll be in the discussion. Confidence tends to win or, at least, not get bullied into bad deals.

Consider These Actions:

- Be the most prepared one in the room. There is no such thing as being over-prepared in negotiations.

- Be the first to propose the structure and price of the deal. You'll worry about leaving something on the table, but the more homework you've done ahead of time, the more confident you'll be that that's not the case.

- Find alternatives that change the conversation. Occasionally, the prospect will dig in their heels. It's not always rational, but to change the conversation, you need to change the focus. Instead of negotiating whether it's a 50/50 split or a 60/40 split, consider the alternatives. Maybe the split is tiered, based on some escalating metric. Or perhaps there's a fixed fee with a different split on the net. When you offer alternatives, it is more likely to move the conversation forward because your prospect sees you're looking for ways for you both to meet your needs and gives them alternative opportunities to still seek a 'win.'

MAKING SIGNING EASY

The legal hurdle is important, but it's a legacy practice that was a lot more relevant to massive enterprise contracts of years ago. Those contracts often made more money on the services and on-premise upgrade charges than they did on the initial sale. It was critical that someone be there to hold the line.

SaaS models have eliminated on-premise software and much of the services bloat that came with it, but the buying process hasn't fully caught up.

Negotiating the terms and conditions of a deal is the absolute worst. There is nothing left to be done that will increase the value in the deal for you. There is only downside. Typically, you're working with lawyers who a) don't understand your product, b) will never touch your product, c) don't know the pains your buyer experiences and thus, have no incentive to help you across the line and d) are willfully blind to business arguments because their job is to kill black swans.

Your customer's legal team could draft the terms and conditions and they'd *still* have changes to it.

SaaS termination clauses often make the worst implausible. It would require both parties staying in an awful, unprofitable relationship for most of the worst-case solutions to come to a head. Use this knowledge as a give to your customer's legal team. Allow them to protect themselves (within reason) against the nightmare scenario if it means you can get to a deal more quickly.

Black swan events exist and can sink you, but if you continually plan for them, you'll move so slowly that the company will run out of oxygen long before the swan's number is drawn. Given the choice of dying now or maybe dying later, you only have one option.

Those issues that will kill you later are often the far-fetched ones dreamt up in the 'plan for worst' minds of lawyers. Should they arise, they would be so massive that you'd lose your company anyhow. In those instances, you'd wind up defending claims by numerous other customers as well. That would cost a ton of money and sink you, just in a different method than originally dreamt by the lawyers.

There is no difference between losing your company once and losing it a hundred times over. Know the terms that, should they occur, are so calamitous (e.g. an employee giving data to competitors or worse) that it doesn't matter what you agree to because you're dead should it ever occur. Push a bit and then give in order to get something in return.

Set agreeable terms, work from your own set of documents, do right by the customer, and keep your funnel flowing and legal bills down.

Consider These Actions:

- Simplify. The longer the terms, the more complicated it looks. Complicated demands legal air cover. Nobody wants to be the one who signed a poor 15-page contract without asking the lawyers to review it. Instead, collect signatures on a standard order form. Focus just on the economic terms. Links within the order form can open the terms and conditions, privacy policies, and service level agreements.

- Post all legal documents on your website. Sunshine is a disinfectant. Should you be confronted with the need to go through legal, you can credibly say that everyone abides by the same legal agreements and that they are publicly posted so everyone is aware of that.

If you absolutely have to work with their legal team:

- Work from *your* terms. Providing the starting point means there will be commonalities amongst all of your customers. When it comes time to sell your business, it will make things a bit less complicated.

- Use common sense. Most issues will never arise and, thus, are rarely worth a protracted battle. The ones worth that time and energy are the ones that contradict your business model (e.g. reuse of aggregated data) or where the situation is unique to this customer and would sink you if it occurs (e.g. assuming liability well above your insured amount). In those cases, push back and be willing to walk away.

RESPECTING LOSSES

Sometimes, it *is* your fault.

Psychologists say that people need to hear roughly five positive things to overcome a single negative remark. Sales presents us with nearly the mirror opposite. It's hard to stay positive when we are so often presented with negative outcomes.

To salve those wounds, it's not uncommon to denigrate your lost prospects.

It's too easy to do, in fact. They're stuck in the past, they don't know how to use computers, they are scared, whatever. There's are numerous reasons people say 'no' and aside from a shortlisted few, all of them can be ridiculed.

While it feels good in the moment, it's destructive. For one thing, you never know when a prospect will come back around and become a customer. But, more importantly, you stunt your learning when you assign blame, no matter how warranted, to your prospect.

It's your job to fit into their reality, not theirs into yours. With every 'no' we should be thankful it wasn't a 'maybe.' And with every 'no' we're being told there is something we could be doing better.

Rather than excusing the result as a byproduct of your prospect's predicament, pull the thread to see what you can do a little differently when presented with the same circumstances again.

You may not always get far but respecting your prospects and customers when you lose them translates into a sustained, positive respect for future ones.

Respect sells.

Consider These Actions:
* Reframe the conversations. It seems silly, but the mindset is different and the responses more meaningful. Instead of asking, "Why didn't they buy?" ask, "What should we have done differently?" Simply asking the question in the other direction keeps salespeople from defensively putting the onus on the prospect.

- Give room for people to vent. Venting is different than denigrating. It's natural to be frustrated but give them that audience in private and out of earshot of the other salespeople. You want to give everyone the chance to unload, but not to the point where it's acceptable for everyone to do so publicly. Set the expectation that negative venting should be done with you and that the group meetings are meant to be reflective and constructive.

- Focus less on the process and the words spoken by the prospect and more on what you didn't understand about them, their internal situation, or their reason for connecting. We lose more deals because we're often blind to our prospect's realities than because we stuck our foot in our mouths or didn't answer a question well. The key is to figure out how you can get inside the head of the next prospect just a little bit better.

IMPROVING WIN RATES VIA POSTMORTEMS

Sales is a numbers game in so much as being a hitter in baseball is a numbers game. Sure, the more at-bats you get the more likely you are to get a single hit. But the batting champion is crowned based on ratio, not quantity. Everything you do has to squeeze one more hit out of your existing number of at-bats. Those at-bats are constrained by your time. You're not going to get more.

The best way to improve your outcomes is to improve your process.

It's incredibly difficult to demo your product, plan the path along which you want your questions to take your prospect, *and* evaluate what can be done better or differently next time.

It's like trying to catch two balls at once. While not impossible, it's rarely done gracefully.

While speaking with a prospect, you're busy listening, contemplating how to respond to what they're saying, and thinking about what else you need to accomplish before your time is up.

It's critical that, at least occasionally, you have someone ride with you to hear what's being said. Someone whose responsibility isn't to talk or to correct your mistakes in the moment, but to provide an objective point of view after the fact in order to tighten up your game.

Evaluations tend to get handled within the regular administrative meetings. Those are rarely meaningful. Doing anything repeatedly creates staleness. Stale meetings are perfunctory and ineffective.

Instead, give postmortems their own time. Pair with one another and do it after a call. Or get everyone to bring their thorniest losses to the table. It's critical they are overly prepared with details, so the loss isn't easily explained away. Celebrate the loss so nobody is afraid to share but find something that will make everyone better in order to keep the meetings meaningful.

The purpose isn't to cast blame, but to thoughtfully learn. The goal is to avoid repeating self-inflicted wounds each time you guide a prospect down your funnel.

Consider These Actions:

- Host tag-team week. Pair your salespeople up to:
  - highlight lines that work and hear others they may not be using themselves;
  - listen to and reflect back the tenor of the prospect's demeanor, not just what's said; and
  - identify questions their partner isn't asking but should.
- Spend as much time as a group conducting postmortems on the wins as the losses. Keep a running list of learnings so it survives beyond the tenure of those in the meetings.
- Structure the postmortem meetings to last only as long as necessary. Lost one deal that week? Then it's a six-minute meeting. Lost ten? Maybe it takes an hour. The point isn't to fill the calendar with meetings, but to make the meetings last as long as they're valuable.
- Track progress. The raw dollars won matter, but the metric is highly susceptible to luck and timing. Keep track of the win percentages over time to focus the attention on getting better at what you're doing, not just doing more of it.

HIRING SALES, IGNORING THE ROLODEX

At some point your investors will push to hire a VP of Sales. (Never mind that they'll be pushing for that too early.) What they're looking for are Jack's magic beans in hopes of climbing the sales beanstalk.

The first inclination of most will be to hire someone who "has the Rolodex." They want someone who can pick up the phone and get the meeting right away.

The mental math is trying to skip the lead-generation process and value propositions in order to get to the proposal. It's a naive approach.

There is <u>no</u> such thing as hiring the Rolodex.

Sales is about providing value and solutions, not calling in favors.

Very, very, very few customers will buy something just because a trusted acquaintance is selling it.

There must be a need. The solution must be the right one. The price must fit the budget. In other words, a sales process has to be undertaken to determine if the fit is right. That holds true regardless of how the lead is generated and how long someone has known the buyer.

At some point, you need to hire someone with experience in a similar type of process (i.e. sales approach, price tag, cycle length, etc.).

But hiring is never easy. Sales is no different.

As with any other function, you must know what you need. Just as you (likely) wouldn't hire a developer who is unfamiliar with the language in which your product is written, you shouldn't hire a sales leader who doesn't have experience with the type of sale you're making.

Making that sales hire requires knowing to whom you're selling, and specifically what makes the sale so challenging. It's not about the latest sales framework, their LinkedIn connections, or what they've sold previously (while it can be instructive, your product will be different). The experience navigating your sales approach is critical. Sometimes it comes with contacts. But a candidate with contacts and without the matching process experience is like throwing (lots) of pennies in a fountain wishing for revenue.

Consider These Actions:
Each of the below are focused on interviewing and hiring that next sales leader. It all comes down to how well they fit your specific sales challenges.

- Identify the type of sale you're making. Are you convincing others of the need or is it well-known? Are you pursuing fewer, bigger deals or more smaller ones? You want someone who has been successful massaging a funnel that looks like yours. Different sales strategies require different skills and mentalities.

- Break down your sales challenges. Where within the funnel is the process breaking now? Generating leads, getting a demo, getting past the group demo, legal, etc.? The right sales leader should be able to address that specific issue with prior work examples and an approach to make it better.

- Know your customer. It doesn't matter what the product was or into what industry someone sold previously, if they were able to connect with and earn the confidence of a similar type of customer with similar types of objections, they can do it again.

- Know your benefits. Not all products are created equally. At RoundPegg, we were selling a solution to fix the invisible (culture). Everyone knows what culture is, but nobody could describe it, let alone say how to improve it. The most effective sales leader we ever worked with had previously sold scents. As in smells. On the face, it may not be obvious, but he was the perfect fit. He was selling something invisible that required a leap of faith (just like selling company culture). Specifically, that if you 'branded' your hotel with a smell, you could increase booked nights.

MOTIVATING BEYOND COIN-OPERATION

How do you motivate your sales team? A bonus? New commission structure?

People are different. We all know that. Yet, too often, founders (and especially investors) harp on the concept of salespeople being coin operated. There is zero upside to entertaining this mentality. It's demeaning and dehumanizing.

Sure, some are. But so are some of your developers and account managers.

Assuming a single motivating factor blinds you to alternative ways to motivate your team.

With no other group will your efforts to motivate be so clearly tied to revenue. Its criticality is obvious. Thus, it's even more imperative that you possess more than one tool for the job.

That's not to say there isn't a kernel of truth about money being a motivator. Everyone is coin operated to varying degrees. But it tends to be the one and only motivating force used with sales.

Salespeople are still human. As people, they need personal validation beyond monetary rewards just like the rest of us: respect, fairness, opportunity, and the leeway to do their best.

To the extent that sales people obsessively focus on compensation is more reflective of the current system than it is of them as individuals. Most companies default to a pay-for-performance structure.

'Making the number' triggers bonuses; missing it triggers two-week notices. Implicit threats are a terrible motivator for most.

When the whole system is set up to evaluate performance around dollars, the natural outcome will be for someone to say they deserve more of it if they're doing well. The system has left employees with only one lever to pull when seeking validation—compensation.

As much as they want authentic appreciation or more responsibility, they also know they're playing within a confined set of rules and that they aren't going to change their manager.

And if there's only one lever at your disposal, you pull it. Years of pulling that lever have cemented management's bias that it's all salespeople care about.

It's a destructive loop that unnecessarily costs you money because you're solving problems with dollars instead of your (free) attention.

Fortunately, this leaves you with a golden opportunity. When everyone is doing the same thing, you can exploit the inefficiency in the market simply by doing things differently (and in this case, cheaper and better). Being human, taking an interest in your salespeople's professional needs, and acknowledging effort in addition to results will set you apart in a market rife with companies hiring slot machines.

While you can't ignore compensation, rewards can come in many forms and, for some, drive better results. It's up to you to identify who is motivated by what.

Consider These Actions:

- Ask questions. Understand your salespeople as intimately as you do other team members. Find out what they want out of their careers, what drives them, and what demotivates. Add it to your personnel scouting reports to bring to your one-on-ones.

- Repeatedly draw connections between every function and the role they play in helping to make sales. Product is needed to differentiate, support creates constructive references, marketing generates the warm leads. Sales is a team effort. Make sure everyone sees that.

- Create communal pools of monetary rewards so everyone shares in the success and does everything they can to support your sales team. The effort others apply to assist sales is a sign of validation and appreciation sales doesn't often see.

OPERATIONS & INVESTMENT

You are at a massive disadvantage.

Your company is facing an industry that has pre-written the rules (likely in a way that isn't intended to give new entrants a leg up). You have no name recognition and no inertia. You have to wear a number of hats, many of which you've never tried on before.

You're not running a company; you're *starting* a company. That difference is stark.

While every function has familiar needs, you don't have the luxury of thinking like the CEO of a company with remotely predictable revenue. You have a time horizon that is measured in weeks or months, not years. Your relationship with time must be different.

Time is your white whale.

Accumulate it wherever you can to ensure the lights are on long enough to find success.

Every dollar buys you a few minutes. There is no distinction between the quality of dollars (yet). A dollar saved spends the same as a dollar earned.

While you're still driving the top line of the financial statements, you must know that what you're doing today isn't what will upset the industry. That's okay. You'll get there, but it requires you survive tomorrow first.

With RoundPegg, I failed to acknowledge the battle was on my doorstep. I tried to build a company with a long view, and it cost us equity and, ultimately, forced us to execute perfectly. And we didn't.

Until you have a moderate grasp of what money will come in the door next month, you must do everything possible to generate a dollar.

It doesn't have to fit squarely into your long-term business model so long as it gives you another chance to move the company forward.

I naively listened to our investors at RoundPegg. Recurring software dollars are sexy, and we wanted to be sexy.

I eschewed offering consulting add-ons because services revenue has a low multiple when valuing a company. What I failed to realize is that we were in the business of buying time and neither your vendors, nor your employees, care whether the dollar that pays them comes from software or services. That unsexy, 'boots on the ground' dollar will keep the lights on and will buy the same amount of time that can generate the next software sale.

Your investors will hate that thinking because it's not increasing your company's on-paper valuation. But that's not your problem (yet). First, you need to get to the point where you're worth something beyond an idea. And you can only solve the problem in front of you. Right now, that's making sure you're giving yourself and your team more time to execute.

Nearly every product requires people to change their behavior. Changing behavior is hard and often requires having boots on the ground to remind people to do things differently. Those boots also lower risk by giving your customers a scapegoat if things go wrong. Companies will pay other companies to absorb blame. Take those dollars.

In the end, every day you buy yourself is another day that you could unlock the repeatable sales process, create the functionality that nobody knew they needed, or find a business model that upends the industry.

Rewriting the industry's rules takes time. Time requires money.

CHANGING THE MARKET TO COMPETE

While your goal should always be to show you're 10x better, it's important to look at all the paths that may lead to that improvement. As the new entrant and the smallest player in the market, your ability to fight toe-to-toe with the entrenched competitors will be limited. They've stared down the tactics available to you before and will do it again if you accept their rules. If you refuse to play by those rules and change the game, you will be far more likely to land a punch that puts them on their heels.

At RoundPegg, my premise was that most psychological assessments have the same general effectiveness (because they do). Thus, taking years to design our own and validate them was a fool's errand that would only waste time and money. Instead, I selected assessments from the public domain (the world's longest four-letter word as far as investors are concerned) that fit the facets crucial to the workplace.

We still needed a good answer for how we could defend against competition, but it wasn't likely to be because we'd found a more effective cheese with which to bait the mousetrap.

One of the most underrated areas to both differentiate within the existing market and to stiff-arm possible new entrants is to change the assumed business model.

Using assessments from the public domain approach meant our per-assessment cost was near zero. We could change how we charged, giving assessments away for free which would allow us to collect more data. The problem people wanted to solve lent itself to know more about everyone on a team. And historically, competitors charged $40-100 per person assessed, limiting the number of people customers wanted to assess.

Our product lay in our ability to aggregate data and automate recommended actions. It allowed us to change the model and attack competitors from a flank where they had less flexibility to address because it put safe revenue at risk.

To be successful, you need to change how customers view the space you want to occupy. You need to do something differently and far better. It need not always fall to your product being the agent of change.

You can create a new industry or transform an existing one by *how* you operate, not just what you've built.

Just because competition exists to sell something doesn't mean they are pricing it or selling it right.

You will have competitors. The longer they've been in the business the more they've convinced the market of the rules of the game. The entrenched players don't want competitors, so naturally the rules are set up to make your life difficult. Don't play by them.

Play by the rules your customer would draw if they were able.

If you can change the game, you can put your competitors on defense and force them to fight by your rules while hamstrung with a legacy cost structure.

Consider These Actions:

- Think on the extremes of your model. Nothing beats free *and* good. Can you do both and extract value elsewhere? Consider:

  - Free. If you had to give your product away for free (not saying you should), how would you do it? Where is value created that can be monetized? Can you get a third-party to pay for it?

  - Strip down your product. What if you only built something that solved one problem? That one thing that gets most people to buy. Would discarding everything else save you enough that you could keep the product viable with a tiny core team?

  - Unlimited. If the competitors charge per X, can you just give your customers unlimited Xs? Most people buy unlimited models not because they're going to be the unprofitable customers for you, but because they want the safety of cost certainty should they need to do more of X. 'Unlimited' is about flexibility, not rational thinking.

- Can you pay your 'customers' instead? Is there a way for you to monetize something your 'customer' produces within your product in a way that your sales pitch becomes, "Why pay for this kind of software? We'll pay you $x thousand every month to use ours in exchange for access to some exhaust data."

FINDING MODEL-MARKET FIT

A laser focus on product-market fit can make you blind to market-model fit. Yet, the two play off one another.

A product that is right enough with a bad business model looks the same as a bad product with a great model. Unless you keep an eye on both, you'll never know which you have.

A traditional product-market fit focus assumes a *Field of Dreams* business model—if you build it, they will come. But there are many other ways on which you can compete as well. Rather than defaulting to the standard price/feature matrices the market has grown accustomed to buying, you have the opportunity to do something that fits your prospect's budget, signing authority, and needs better.

A startup's biggest advantage is flexibility. Use it to test business models.

Every competitor's business model has a weakness—a reason a segment of customers will churn. Can you build your model around their weakness?

For example, if the competition requires a contract, can you go month-to-month? If they require the customer license their own data, can you guarantee its confidentiality? If they charge per seat, can you provide an unlimited use?

Model differentiation can't be copied nearly as quickly as feature differentiation.

Further, the model can dictate your terms and conditions, which gives you permission to do things with data that entrenched competitors could only wish to do.

It becomes nearly impossible for large competitors to renegotiate terms after having made the sale and set up an entire employee ecosystem around supporting and renewing the customer. The risk of change is too great, and risk is the one thing around which large companies have evolved to stamp out.

Consider These Actions:
- Try the extremes. How can you give your product away for free? Is there exhaust data that you can turn around and sell in the aggregate to others in order to fully subsidize your intended market? Conversely, is there an

insight or are there data in your product that you could expose to your customers that get them to pay ten times what the market is currently bearing? Probably not, but the extremes can help expose the right questions.

- Think like your customer. What about the existing business models doesn't work for them? There is a more creative solution if you can better understand where they find value, how the buyers are evaluated in their job, when budgets are set, and how the horse-trading works prior to the budgets being finalized.

- Believe there's always another way. You may not have found it yet, but you can't let yourself stop looking. If it requires breaking your core product up into a dozen pieces and selling them all individually, you should explore that.

MODELING YOUR BUSINESS

'Pro Forma' may be Latin for bullshit. Everyone knows it, but it's still critical to investment.

Where entrepreneurs go wrong is working on the assumption that the revenue matters most.

The purpose of a financial model for a company with little to no revenue is to show that you understand how you compete for the long haul, how to monetize customers, and how to manage the costs needed to support them. It's about showing the relationship between revenue and expense.

You have to show you have a plan for how to generate a dollar and that you understand the cost of each of those dollars generated.

The growth curve tends to be the only component on which many founders focus. Investors perpetuate the need to 'see the confidence' that you'll be generating $100 million in five years. Founders buy into it and build the financial models to satisfy it. While seemingly harmless, it hurts the founder by making it look as though you don't know your business.

The data show that roughly one in every 3,000 companies started this year will hit that 9-figure mark in *six* years. It's just not happening.

You need to show you understand the business you're in, not the charade in which you participate. Your model is your path to highlight your knowledge of the levers you have to pull to get there.

So, where do you start? The top-down approach (i.e. it's a 100-bazillion dollar market and if we can just get 1%, we're worth a bazillion dollars!) is thankfully long dead. But the bottom-up approach is hard, takes a lot of time, and feels small.

It's not fun to build because everything has a dependency.

Revenue requires onboarding a new customer, which requires a sale, which requires a product, which requires money, which requires a sale, etc. It's like a roundabout without an obvious onramp.

Starting from the bottom up will give you a more realistic approach. It will force you to think about the little things that have to happen in order to close a deal and what it takes to keep the revenue coming. It becomes a spreadsheet that tells you how you should spend your days and where you should prioritize.

While you still need to show investors that you believe in the nine-figure potential of your company, you don't have to look naive in the process. While the only guarantee you can give is that your model will be wrong, you'll be able to quantitatively communicate what are the keys to success and where you need to invest in order to build muscle.

Consider These Actions:
Rather than list out broad ideas, below is an approach to help you think more holistically about your model.

- **People.** Time is your constraint. Before you do anything, calculate the different components of someone's job and how much time each task takes in order to determine how many customers each can service. Once you know how many customers (or prospects) one head can handle, you will have a better understanding of what your headcount growth plan needs to be if you were to simply grow organically.

- **Product I.** If you don't yet have a salable product, you need to calculate the cost just to get to that point. For example, what are the requirements for the smallest product you can sell? How long will it take? How many people are needed to build it in that amount of time? How much will they cost? Then double it. Seriously.

- **Leads.** To make a sale, you need leads. How are yours acquired? If they are done by people, calculate how many hours a lead gen person has in a given day and how many contacts they can make in that time. What're the steps involved in generating that lead and the success rate at each step? Add to it the cost to acquire contact lists, marketing, etc. to get you the cost per lead.

- **Sales.** The sales funnel leaks all the way down. Understand the process it takes to close a deal and estimate the leakage you encounter at each step (e.g. your funnel may require an individual demo, group demo, second group demo, proposal, procurement, and legal stage before determining a win or loss). Your constraint is the number of demos and follow ups one sales rep can perform in a given time period. If a demo is an hour and there's 30-minutes of prep on the front end and 30-minutes of follow up on the back, then doing more than two or three in a day is unrealistic. (If you forecast to close more than a sixth of your pipeline, consider adding more leakage in the funnel.)

- **Support.** New customers require onboarding and support. Their need should taper over time, but your account managers can only onboard so many new customers in a given week while still maintaining an acceptable level of service for existing customers. How much time will it take to onboard and train a customer? How many months until they're comfortable independently using your product? How much support is needed after they've learned the system?

- **Product II.** Once you have customers, you need to dedicate time to fixing bugs and refining the user experience. For every new customer, some amount of development time will be needed to service their requests. To simplify matters, estimate what percentage of time will be spent between existing support and new features. Estimate development growth (i.e. new feature builds) as a function of revenue so you can keep costs in line.

- **Expenses.** Headcount will be 70% of your expense, so by understanding the capacity of each role above. you're more than halfway home. Most costs will be variable based on headcount or customer count. Maintain a running tally of headcount and customer count. Then, link the remaining expenses as a multiple of each (e.g. office leases are a function of headcount while legal expenses are a function of customer count).

- **Curve bending.** The downside of the approach above is that it assumes everything is linear. All you have to do to generate more revenue is add more sales reps. Obviously, it's not that easy. Building in onboarding time for new heads (decrease efficiency and effectiveness) will better reflect reality. Similarly, the number of customers a development team can support may increase as the overlap of bugs and requests becomes greater and the product improves. It doesn't feel elegant but have a separate sheet that bends curves based on various triggers (e.g. time-based curves that show efficiencies learned or headcount-based curves that bend efficiency via specialization). This is slightly more accurate and helps you reach the investor community's magic numbers.

PRICING TO MAXIMIZE REVENUE

B2B SaaS deals, regardless of size, involve a lot more psychology and flexibility than a typical B2C purchase.

You're asking someone to buy something for annual price that falls between a used car and a new house. The confidence we have in our pricing strategy is already shaky before considering the magnitude of the cost.

But when you create value for your customer, you are entitled to extract a piece for yourself.

B2B negotiations are psychological minefields for those approaching it for the first time. You need support in order to stand your ground on price as negotiations begin. How you price and package can help.

There are multiple paths to price discrimination (i.e. get more revenue from those who see more value). Some considerations for each include:

Bundling
There is a reason you see the three-to five-columned pricing sheets these days. They work.

They work for the customer who is sensitive to paying for things they don't need, and they work for you because you're able to extract revenue from multiple points along a customer's value spectrum.

Bundling also prevents your prospect from line-item vetoing specific pieces to negotiate downward. They can choose A, B, C, or D but not A and a half.

The reason to bundle is to allow you to align your price with both actual and perceived value. Some customers get more value from your product than others. If they do, you should be rewarded for providing that value.

If the value your product creates is a dial (i.e. if it's possible for one person to get a little bit and another a ton), then you can price discriminate based on the specific features that create each of those value points.

If the entirety of the value you create is a switch (i.e. all value is extracted just by using the main functionality), then you are forced to price discriminate via other methods, like the number of users, the level of service provided, etc.

There are downsides to them all. Knowing them allows you to pick the one that's right for your industry.

Limiting Features
Determining where the value/feature breaks are is not always obvious. It requires knowing the different use cases and going through the exercise of slowly taking one feature after another away to determine when customers start threatening to cancel. Those screams dictate your bundle breaks.

Tracking usage metrics is critical for a number of reasons, but with respect to pricing, it is your best starting point for hearing the screams without actually taking the features away from a user. Even better, it can help save you the expensive long-term costs to build and support complex permission matrices.

Restricting Users
Sometimes, the pain you solve is individualized (e.g. CRMs). While add-on features can make CRMs more valuable, the primary value is derived by discrete core functionality of simply storing everyone who needs to be contacted and when. These are the occasions when throttling users can be more useful to maximize revenue.

The downside is that per-seat pricing creates a misaligned incentive between you and your customer.

Most SaaS products make money on retention. Per-seat pricing provides an incentive for organizations to limit who can use your product because it keeps their costs down.

Restricting use lowers your customer's switching costs, making it easier to leave you.

The more who use, the more who have to get retrained, the more who will complain, and the more who are likely to tell you about the one thing that needs changing in order to keep the account. That friction is valuable to your retention.

Varying Service Level
Some customers light your time on fire. Others never reach out. The cost difference between the two is glaring.

Throttling service rarely works unless you can price discriminate enough to justify hiring a new dedicated position to service a singular customer.

From a cost perspective it can make sense to discriminate based on service. It costs more to manage an instant service queue via phone than it does an asynchronous queue via e-mail.

But help is help. And help is costly.

Your inclination will *always* be to help. And your priority is to keep your customer happy in order to get them to pay again next month. The reality is that you won't follow your service level promises and everyone will get great service whether or not they pay for it. So just make everyone pay for it and sell it as a benefit.

Customer Size
The pricing at Distillery Solutions was based on a distillery's production volume. Logically, it made sense. The bigger the producer, the more value they were getting from the software.

But how do you respond to someone who asks, 'why am I paying twice what the distiller next door is paying for the exact same report just because I've run my business better and been able to grow?'

Every package sold had the same feature set, the only difference was the customer's size. The model worked, but it was sloppy. It was a legacy model, dictated by the product's ability to do one thing and one thing well: produce a monthly government-mandated report. There were ways to discriminate based on the types of products sold (e.g. if they bundled items), but the product wasn't flexible enough to extract that value from the core.

The lesson learned was that the product design shouldn't dictate the business model. Instead, we would have done better had we carved out the requested features in order to add extra value based on what our customer was selling, instead of how much they sold. We'd have gotten to the same place (bigger customers usually sell a broader selection of products) without raising eyebrows and given our competitors an opportunity to pounce.

Consider These Actions:
- Know why people buy. What are you solving? Pricing can get overly complex very quickly. If you're bundling or have a tiered approach, center each package around the *one* thing that drives most of the value. More stuff isn't always more valuable.
- Know how you want to be positioned. Being the best and cheapest is excellent if your costs are next to nothing. But that's a tough perch from

which to direct a business. When you know how you want to compete, it makes pricing a little clearer. Not being the low-cost solution is actually a great position. Relish it but fulfill the promise.

- Track product use to know what value is being extracted and by whom. Sell the value. Optimizing revenue requires monetizing all the small scraps of value produced.

DE-RISKING OPERATIONS

You are in the risk-mitigation business.

Your investors want to place bets on companies with no risk and massive reward. Your customers want to be assured that you won't make them look bad and will be in business this time next year. Your employees want an assurance that the next payroll will be met.

These are your bosses. All of them are telling you to avoid unnecessary risk.

As the company's steward, you have to navigate the path that leads to riches without triggering the booby traps that launch the spiked javelins or expose the hole with the ravenous lion waiting at the bottom.

This is more than analyzing each decision as to which provides the greatest reward for the amount of risk. It requires looking at your company differently. It demands squeezing perceived risk out of each relationship.

Thinking as Investor
The challenge we have as entrepreneurs is that we don't understand what a worst-case scenario looks like. That forecast we crafted feels infinitely reasonable and we'll insist it's conservative. Yet we'll miss by half.

Your ability to eliminate risk from the investor perspective is to hit your numbers.

You need to know what you can achieve with 90% certainty. If you know the top line with that precision—even if it's modest—you build their confidence in you and the business. It opens doors to further investment because they *want* to, not because they have to. It pushes the decision to 'bring in adult supervision.' By hitting your metrics, you give the investors' confidence that money won't run out any sooner than forecasted. You're protecting your investment by protecting theirs.

Thinking as Competitor
How would you sell against your company? What are the weaknesses you would exploit to scare a prospect about what you're doing and what you may do in the future?

You're not in control of the narrative others tell, nor will you always know what they're saying. If they've found a play that works, they're going to keep running it until you figure out how to stop it. Each time they run it and win, you lose money. So why not game plan for it before they use it against you?

When I first started at Distillery Solutions, there was one imposing competitor and the sales teams would duke it out on just about every deal. The stories the competition told about how we charged, the value we brought, and how we operated weren't always accurate, but there was enough of a grain of truth to them that they were believable.

We had to eliminate the grains of truth.

First, we had a business model that had 13 different pricing tiers. The logic was sound—to help those just starting out control their costs. But the reality was that there was a variable price every month based on their average production. Nobody could plan their expenses, and that outflow of cash didn't match up with their sales receipts.

Our competitor, wisely, talked up his flat-rate pricing. "You will pay $x forever. It doesn't matter if you produce a bottle of whiskey or a million." He took advantage of everyone's optimism and highlighted that they wouldn't "be punished" for being successful.

Simple. Appealing. Forecastable.

Not to mention it required no internal overhead for him to update billing each month.

We flattened things out into three tiers so as not to lose those who weren't price sensitive and offered to lock distilleries into a price for life. Join when you're small and you will never jump a tier. In an industry that's exploding, you will have those who get big, but revenue growth was coming from more producers rather than the small ones getting big.

Offering a price for life caused us to lose out on capturing revenue from a few major success stories, but it won far more deals. Everyone dreamt of being big and this allowed them to hold that dream without paying for it.

It eliminated the competition's key selling point and gave us six months of open road.

Before long, we started hearing (false) stories about how our customers couldn't extract their data and, thus, didn't own it. To counter, we simply made the export buttons bigger and more colorful. In the months it took to recognize his new tactic though, we lost sales.

This was the dance we played until we started getting in front of our weaknesses and solving them with product changes, pricing updates, added headcount, etc. It wasn't until we could objectively acknowledge our weaknesses that we truly got strong.

Thinking as Employer
What would happen if you lost an employee this afternoon? People aren't interchangeable, and some are far more valuable than others. But even the lowest performers know something that will take some time to reveal or to replicate.

You need to know who holds pivotal knowledge and what it is.

Your protection to minimize flight risk is to create the processes that safeguards your investment. Those processes should extract and spread knowledge amongst the rest of the team. While not everyone needs to know everything, everything should have multiple owners holding overlapping chunks.

At the same time, you have to take away reasons someone possessing difficult-to-replicate value will leave. The reasons people leave typically revolve around not feeling appreciated, not having enough opportunity, or simply wanting to run from dysfunction. Being proactive with rewards and recognition and constantly seeking ways to make things run more smoothly, go a long way to remove the excuse to look for another job.

Thinking as Employee
The asymmetry in the employment process just isn't fair. An employee needs to be on guard to fend off risk because the cost to them is so much greater.

A company can weather an employee departure because that represents $1/x$ the value created walking out the door. (X could be the number of employees or fewer, but the point is that it's not 100%.) When an employee loses their salary, they lose 100% of it. They need to hustle to find a replacement revenue stream and few companies hire quickly enough to align with a severance period.

The anxiety this causes leads them to read into every communication (or lack thereof). Acknowledging this helps you realize why they are always trying to read the tea leaves based on customer acquisition, churn, investor sentiment, etc. Their first priority is, as it should be, to care for themselves and their family.

Eliminating risk from the employee's perspective is possible with aggressive transparency. Your employees have a right to know where the company stands; how much cash is left, what assumptions are being made to get to the next round of investment (or, better, customer acquisition), and what expenses are the first to go. You hired them because they're smart. Smart people arrive at conclusions on their own. Give them the data to make those decisions so they aren't fabricating 'what ifs' that are rarely optimistic.

The winds are already at your back to retain people. (Looking for a new job is a hassle. Inertia is rough to overcome.) If you can keep them reasonably satisfied, they typically won't seek greener pastures.

Thinking as Customer
The greatest risk you pose to a customer is making them look bad. Presumably the customer purchased your product because you make her job easier. The expectation is that the job will get done and get done well. Therefore, there is little room for unexpected upside. A bug, being down, or finding out you lack an assumed feature creates a loser situation for your customer. New products present a real but unknown downside.

Acknowledging these risks beforehand shows your prospect you're aware of their situation. Addressing reality head on can build their confidence in your ability to hit the best-case scenario.

Consider These Actions:
- Rotate responsibilities. There are advantages gained by allowing someone to go deep in a particular role. But the downside is they're the only one who knows it. Shift responsibilities periodically so everyone has a little bit of knowledge about a lot. Should they leave, you're more likely to have someone who knows most of what they took with them.
- Learn to offboard. Few companies take the time to properly offboard. Get as much of their knowledge before they leave as possible. Have them pair with others. Have them craft a list of things they wanted to change, or reasons things haven't gotten done or reasons things will explode.
- Hire slowly. It's always easier to scale up than down.

GAINING TIME BY OPTIMIZING JOBS

Companies get to profitability by growing revenue.

But with most of the expense tied up people, finding cost-efficient processes can most easily create long-term success. Not only does it create margin, but also a competitive advantage that isn't easily replicated.

When everyone is working together and communicating well, pulling hard in a (relatively) similar direction, and not wasting time with tedious tasks, you have a team that can vastly out-produce companies with many times more employees.

Profits tend to follow highly functioning teams.

Getting more out of employees is often about aligning rewards and effort. The unsung hero of motivation is removing the worst parts of someone's job. Engaging someone is about trying to find ways to help them do more of the things that give them energy and take away as many of those that don't.

If you asked someone to hire for a new junior position in their department the job description will consist of all the unpleasant things the person writing the job description doesn't want to do.

And that should become your starting point to find efficiencies.

Amongst that list are things that probably aren't adding enough value relative to the effort involved. Eliminate them.

Likely portions are important and can't be eliminated but just take way too long. Optimize those. Find ways to remove a step in the process.

And some are too important to eliminate but don't have obvious inefficiencies. Those are the ones that make it 'a job,' but you can trade retaining those for eliminating and optimizing the others.

It's unrealistic to say everyone should only work on the things they love. You don't have enough people or even the right people for that. Instead, acknowledge that some tasks are not fun, but that they are vital, and reinforce your desire to help make the employee's job better by changing the components you can.

As an example, our team of inside salespeople was making roughly 25-30 calls per day. In an era where actually speaking on the phone is becoming less common, it meant they were leaving at least 22 voicemails per day. Each voicemail was nearly identical to the last. Each voicemail required sitting through the outgoing message and listening to the pleasantly vanilla female voice announce the same instructions about what to do after recording the message.

It was neither difficult nor a long process—roughly 90-seconds from the time the voicemail began to the time the rep hung up.

But it was awful.

You could hear the energy drain from their voices as the day wore on. You could feel the weight they shouldered as they trudged into our calling booths. This was a chore.

I'd never seen happiness in the workplace like I did when someone on the team found software that would automatically leave voicemails (that they'd pre-recorded in their own voice) for them based on which number they pressed.

They each recorded a handful of high energy, smiling voicemails and that was it. They didn't have to leave another message. They saved themselves only about twenty minutes a day (they still had to listen for the beep first) but they didn't feel like they were doing a job that, literally, could be done by a tape recorder.

They started making more calls and getting more responses because it didn't sound like they were reading a hostage note on every voicemail. It created a virtuous cycle where the negative task was made tolerable which led to more positive results.

I'm 100% convinced they'd have been willing to pay for the software out of their own pockets and then some, if asked. Instead, they put in more effort because the job was more tolerable.

Ask your team what they hate doing and sometimes you can find ways to unlock more productivity via very simple (and inexpensive) things.

Consider These Actions:

- Be inquisitive. Always ask why things are done the way they are. Often, there's not a good reason for it other than it's the way it's always been done. Have everyone walk you through the process they have for generating a lead, onboarding a new customer, responding to support tickets, etc. There are always a few extra hours waiting to be better utilized each week. This is how you buy time. Saving someone an hour a week will tally up to 7 full workdays by the end of the year.

- Start with all the things that are done, every day without fail. If something is done every day, it becomes tiresome. Any chance to shave a little time and effort in these areas will add up quickly.

- Create the expectation that everyone should look for ways to save themselves time. When you hear a complaint, ask how they'd fix it. Constantly ask what can be done better and more efficiently. Make noise about changing a process that drives efficiency. Nothing is too little to celebrate. Be careful to never shoot down ideas. It may not be right (or good) but don't kill the effort. Instead see what's right in it and ask for refinements.

DECIDING TO RAISE

Because most of us didn't win the trust-fund lottery, we often find ourselves needing to raise money to pay rent. Securing equity investment is an unfair 'reward' for being willing to take the risk of forgoing an income in order to prove ourselves.

Thus, the treadmill starts. Now, in order to make what you'd likely earn from selling your bootstrapped company, you have to sell for 3-5x the amount. One slip and the company must sell for 10-20x the bootstrapped number. Two slips and you likely won't see a dollar.

Avoiding these slips requires facing the investment with more gravitas. It's not the goal nor does it allow you to exhale. There is no further guarantee of future funding so it's not a pain reliever. If anything, you've doubled down on the need to execute and play the match perfectly.

The slips will come. But they may be fewer and farther between if you are able to change your mindset following the investment. Doing so can help you recognize the falls prior to the ground rushing up and hitting you in the face.

It starts with changing the relationship to the invested money.

Most importantly, recognize that an investment into your company is a bet on what you *will* achieve, not a reward for what you have achieved.

Then, tactically, think of the investment as a line of credit. With a line of credit you are actively aware of your need to be able to service the debt once you draw upon it. You make decisions differently. If you had to pay the investment amount back, could you do it?

The easiest way to answer that is whether you know how you're going to generate revenue from the investment. Obviously, if you could borrow a dollar and turn it into two, you'd do that every day. But you're not there yet. Can you change the mindset to translate investment into revenue? Even if it's turning a dollar into a dime, it's a start.

For example, if you're looking at office space, you may find yourself thinking, "it's only an extra $2,000/mo. for this nice office space and we have a million in the bank."

Instead, consider whether you will we be able to generate more than that simply by being in a different office. The answer may be yes. It's not a vow of poverty, but a way of thinking that gets you in the mindset of being an owner who has personally secured the line of credit.

The trap of thinking about it as a pool of money that rewarded your success to date is that you set yourself up for getting clobbered in the next round.

This isn't to say that you shouldn't raise venture money, but that it should be approached cautiously.

In general, you want to prove that with the first dollar invested you can turn it into a dime. The second dollar that comes in should generate a quarter, the third another dollar, and the fourth many dollars.

Money can buy you time. But that time is only valuable when you use it to solve how to buy more money.

Capital doesn't care if you don't execute. In fact, institutional investors can add to their stake when you don't (but just once or twice).

Capital only cares if you generate a return.

Consider These Actions:

- Bootstrap as long as possible. If you have a product, start selling it. You may still wind up having to raise, but you may also give yourself the freedom of not needing to do so.

- See everything in outcomes. Investment should lead to specific economic outcomes. How you get there could be any number of paths. Investment buys the time to explore those paths. Your job is to see which path can provide the best return on the invested dollar.

- Be brutally frugal. Everything takes twice as long and costs twice as much. You'll hear it constantly. Plan for that. If your hiring plan calls for doubling this year, grow 50%. Run a little slower than you think is required so you buy yourself the freedom to make a mistake or two along the way.

FUNDRAISE TODAY

Should you decide to raise funds by selling equity in your company, you need to start today. Fundraising requires a relationship though. How frequently do you give money to the (adult-sized) solicitors who knock on your door and ask you're your contribution? Your fundraising effort shouldn't look like that.

Investors need to know you and need proof that your company is as riskless as possible. The best response you can give to the latter is to create momentum.

Creating a relationship backed by momentum requires time.

Growth rates and progress are seductive and create time sensitivity (the more you grow the more expensive you get, and you inch closer to financial autonomy, the ultimate leverage point). You can only show momentum when you have repeated contact with the investor. Momentum is the line between the dots on your graph from one touchpoint to the next.

Everyone needs a reason to put a term sheet on the table. Without competition—even just the fear of missing out—there is no reason to invest until the very last minute when they have you on the ropes to get a better deal.

With two points, people can draw a line and extend it further to see where you'll be next. With a single point, that line can slope in any direction based on their view of you.

Set the first point today. It'll never be lower and further to the left – which is actually a good thing. You can't help but show momentum in the next conversation.

By not putting yourself on the line today, you've paid your investors a few hundred to a few thousand dollars in equity. Was it worth it?

Consider These Actions:
* See *Fundraise Like Sales* and start creating a top 150 targets. Introduce yourself.
* Ask questions and get interested in the expertise the investor's hold. It's an ego boost but, if you can get insights into the challenges you face, also provides you a dose of value in exchange for the time you invest.

- Create a 6-9-month content calendar. Identify the announcements you want to make to your investor pool every few weeks. Some can be things that have already happened but where the announcement is delayed in order to maximize impact. The key is that every couple weeks you have something of real import to announce, not just an update to your four KPIs. It creates a story. Stories create emotions. Emotions invest.

FUNDRAISE LIKE SALES

The opportunity cost to fundraising is too often lost. Every hour you focus on investors is an hour you could have spent finding non-dilutive money (revenue).

Unfortunately, that time you spend raising money does little to increase the value of your company. Should you land money, it's still only your ability to execute that creates value. The conversations to reach that point help you tell a story, but not one that will resonate with people who buy your product. The justifications we tell ourselves as to the value of raising rarely pans out.

We are raising money to buy ourselves time. That's it.

Thus, your goal should be (and is) to spend as little time on it as possible. The sooner you get it done, the sooner you can get back to creating value.

But rarely is a strategy to shortcut the process ever put in place.

When heading down the fundraising path, treat it like you would sales.

Put in the sweat upfront to qualify your prospects so you can increase your batting average.

When it comes to sales, we spend months, even years, thinking about our customer. Who they are, what they need, what they will pay, etc.?

While raising money for RoundPegg, we talked to nearly 100 investors before closing our first round. It was an all-encompassing waste of time. Not because investors couldn't see the vision, but because we didn't do anything at all to understand the people to whom we were talking.

We took meetings with anyone who would say yes. A hole in the calendar and a website that qualified them as investors was about all it took for us to be there. Some call that hustle. I now look at that and call it naively stupid.

The atrocious math behind an investor's year does not favor the entrepreneur. Nor should it. Hearing only three pitches a week puts the number of prospective investments available to the VC north of 150 a year. Each partner can realistically juggle six board seats or so. So, in the typical seven-year lifecycle of the fund where the bets are placed in the first four years, you can estimate that one deal a year will get funded.

1%.

Your odds of getting funded are that small.

That's why you have to target investors with the same ferocity and focus that you target prospects. If you double your odds to 2% then you save 50 meetings which, being generous, buys you 25 full days (at no cost). You are buying yourself an extra month by putting a few day's effort in on the front end to understand who will be more likely to invest in you.

This doesn't make fundraising easier; simply more efficient.

Consider These Actions:
Fortunately, there are now lists available that will help you see (almost) the entirety of the VC universe. Start there and winnow down. Filter by:

- Stage: Identify those who invest in your stage. There's no use (yet) getting in front of the larger investors. 'Getting on their radar' can be done via email updates.

- Industry: Stay broad (your top three or four industries around which you could slot yourself) but focus on those who have invested in your industry before.

- Location: While there is no reason to eliminate an investor based on their location, make sure those left on your list have invested outside their own backyard. Most like to be able to drive to visit their money, even if they won't admit it.

- Partner history: Don't just approach any partner. Find one that has made money in your space before or someone who has been on the board of a company that solved a similar operational challenge.
  - Founding companies: Partners who have started companies in your vertical can be enormously valuable. Every one of the other partners will be looking to them as the expert and will follow their lead. So, start by engaging them.
  - Investment success: If an investor has turned a buck into five or ten investing in a specific niche, the odds are they'll try to do so again. If nothing else, they'll have seen what worked and what didn't in your particular space. Curb the hubris even more than normal and use those opportunities to walk out with more knowledge than you came in. Even if you don't get an investment, you should be

able to hear the backstory of growth and learn a few things not to do.

- Alumni connections: It's painful to admit, but there is a 'clubbiness' within the investor-entrepreneur relationship. Sharing an 'elite' affiliation is another signal you're worthy of consideration.

- Other affiliations: Non-profit boards, personal interests, speaking panels, etc. all indicate where a partner's interests lie. Play to their interests.

DESIGNING THE PITCH EXPERIENCE

Because investors put money into less than 1% of the companies they meet in a given year, it's natural that their default position is 'What's wrong with this company?' The investor needs to quickly identify the best, so they are spending their limited time on the most interesting opportunities.

Your job is to change their thinking as quickly as possible.

Fortunately, they're human. Not only must you show there is a huge pot of gold at the end of the rainbow and that you've eliminated an enormous amount of risk already, but you have to entertain.

You are the monkey grinding that organ. Embrace it.

Consider These Actions:

- Tell a story. The first minute of your presentation is the most important. If you lose them early, you've lost them entirely.

  Nearly everyone will start with what their company does, followed by the problem.

  Is there a counter-intuitive story that is interesting and highlights the need for what you do? For example, one company monitored traffic patterns to help move traffic more efficiently. Rather than starting with a vision of no traffic jams and stating the problem is that stop lights are updated with new traffic data every five years, they told a story of the first stop light. It was manned by a traffic cop sitting atop a tower on the side of the road. It was America's first smart light. This was the one instance where technology today is dumber than it was 140 years ago.

- Show a pattern. Has the 'evolution' you're creating already happened in an adjacent industry? Show it. It makes it more likely to happen again, reducing risk. If you can show you're merely copying/pasting the playbook from another industry with look-a-like circumstances, then they don't have to bet on your ability to predict the future, just on your ability to execute. As hard as the latter is, it's far easier than the former.

- Get pithy. The most difficult part of pitching your company is figuring out what not to say.

Creating 100 slides and talking for hours is easy. Creating the top ten vital points you want to make and constructing a cohesive conversation is not. Open your current deck right now and cut 70% of it. Then give yourself a one-in-one-out mandate. Have a new idea, new anecdote, or new slide? Take another out.

- Record yourself. It's awful and uncomfortable to hear yourself speak, but you'll hear what your audience is hearing instead of what you intend to say. The difference between what you're trying to say and what gets heard is often huge. Be your own audience. Entertain yourself.

- Stop talking about the problem. The inclination of many entrepreneurs is to walk others (particularly investors) along the path. You want to prove you're capable of adjusting when you have new information and you want to prove you're smart. It's natural. It's also tedious, irrelevant, and boring.

  The juicy stuff is the solution. Nobody buys problems. People buy solutions.

- Be stunningly honest. Every business is different. And every startup faces different challenges. You know your biggest challenges. Hit them head-on in the presentation.

  Your audience is already thinking them. It's a steady low-level hum in their head that distracts them from what you're actually saying. It's better to get those challenges out there and have the chance to address them than to let them go unsaid and hope the investor doesn't see them. Investors are smart and have seen thousands of presentations. You aren't going to fool them.

- Get them involved. Everyone wants the pitch to be a conversation. It's a more natural way of communicating. Yet we default to putting a presentation up on a screen that puts our audience into a passive viewing state.

  If you want a conversation, identify natural breaks where you can pose a question. It helps to know their background so you can make the question more relevant. For example, "You invested in [xyz], which has taken a similar approach. What did you learn from them in that process?"

- Focus their attention. People can't do two things at once.

When you are projecting your slides and talking to them simultaneously your audience is either reading or listening. Not both.

If you need a visual during your presentation, use pictures. A deck with words is a leave behind.

- Show don't tell. If you have a product, you need to spend the time you have together playing with it. You wouldn't buy a house without walking through it and imagining yourself waking up there in the morning. Investing five or six zeroes into something requires more than reading a summary. You need to viscerally 'feel' what it's like. Give your audience that experience in order to give yourself the chance to get the investment.

- Introduce yourself, not just your product. Without a lot of traction, you are your product. You've put so much thought and effort into it that you can't tell the two apart any longer. The downside is that you focus on the product at the expense of yourself. They need to know you. Ideas are a dime a dozen and are worthless without execution. Show them you know how to execute with past examples.

  - Why are you the one to execute?

  - What have you done before that will prove you can do it again?

  - What makes you special?

  - Why would they want to invest in you versus the next person to come along with the same idea?

  Treat the pitch like a job interview where you come prepared with examples of how you've made things happen, led others to do something great, or overcome some adversity. Everyone loves stories and everyone wants to back winners. Your job is to show why you are a winner, not just why your product is a winner.

- Design the questions you want. Leave objections unanswered. It facilitates a conversation. If you don't leave any questions on the table, you don't leave the door open for a back and forth. Every question has a natural entry into the conversation, draw them out if you don't get it when you expect.

- Create multiple overviews. Have a variety of overviews based on what stage you're in with the investment process. Sending the full pitch isn't appropriate prior to meeting someone, just as sending the one-liner isn't after meeting the full partnership group.

  - Introduction – a two- to three-sentence overview someone else can forward
  - 1st meeting ask – a one-page overview (with lots of whitespace)
  - 1st meeting – the story deck
  - 1st meeting leave behind – the deck with the talk track
  - 2nd meeting ask – the updated progress charts and a little more detail on the industry

PITCHING FOR PATTERN RECOGNITION

Most investors are incredibly skilled at pattern recognition. They look for solutions that tend to fit market dynamics they've previously seen exploited. Your solution then, can sometimes be a negative. Most firsts don't follow easily recognized patterns.

Your odds of getting funded are already low. Help yourself by identifying patterns that you follow.

As often as "We're the [xyz] of ABC" is derided, it serves a massive purpose. It gives investors a framework upon which your concept can be evaluated. That is, can this product be sold and see growth like this other highly successful company? Often, the answer is no, but at least there is a method against which to evaluate.

It isn't easy to find the go-to market model that you'll be able to copy/paste, but the effort of looking is worth the time invested. It could save you dozens of meetings (i.e. give you back weeks of time).

More critically, it can help you identify the challenges you'll have to overcome. Finding a market that faces similar pressures to change and a buyer with similar budget considerations, similar power structures, etc. will expose you to how others have tried to solve them.

At RoundPegg, I failed to find a match. It felt like time poorly spent and I opted for an easy comparison, not a useful one. Misidentifying the approach meant we learned lessons over the following year that I should have learned in days upfront.

We sold into the HR space and had a strategic solution. It affected every person within an organization. The mistake I made was saying that our approach would be similar to SuccessFactors, at the time one of the select few HR technology successes. Just as SuccessFactors created a rigorous, proactive approach to employee performance evaluation and improvement cycle, we were doing the same for company culture.

Wrong.

While performance reviews are strategic, SuccessFactors was simply digitizing the process. Every HR technology success to that point (and sadly, still today) have been digitization projects, taking existing offline behavior and moving it online (classifieds, Rolodexes, resumes, etc.).

Despite saying we were 'SuccessFactors for Culture,' the connection wasn't credible. Everyone knew there was a budget of time and dollars allocated to performance evaluations, as well as a forcing mechanism for action (promotions/raises). We were selling something that had no strategic budget.

Case in point: we lost a deal when the budget was allocated toward weekly summer ice-cream socials instead.

Raising a dollar was a constant struggle. We didn't match any pattern where an investor could road test the idea and acknowledge it might work.

Consider These Actions:

- Research. There is no substitute for finding another company that found success doing something akin to what you're doing. You will have nailed it if you can match based on how and why people buy, how the pricing structure works, and where the power dynamics lie.
- Ask investors where they see a similar pattern. Get them thinking along your lines and trying to solve the same problems you are. They may find a better answer than your own. If they start to get excited, you're a few steps ahead of all the other fundable companies out there.
- Find a parallel for the problem. The problem is what you're solving, not necessarily the industry.

MINIMIZING THE PERCEIVED RISK

Most venture investors have an aversion to risk.

It stands to reason. Funds are raised on the wallets of wealthy, limited partners. Those LPs entrust pieces of their fortunes to a venture partner tasked with making intelligent decisions, not gambling it away on needlessly risky investments.

Odds are that you aren't doing nearly enough to minimize the risk you present.

In order to raise money, you need to show there's a big market, opportunity to capture a chunk of it, _and_ that you are more likely than not to do so (i.e. you are not a risky bet). Typically, we only focus on the first two, but every slide you show should prove the latter.

Your goal is to show that you are high reward, minimal risk.

Areas of risk are manifold, but you need to systematically address each one. Amongst a slew of others, consider:

Team risk
* Are you and your co-founders smart enough?
* Do you hustle?
* Can you execute?
* Can you get others to execute?
* Are you open-minded enough to pivot when things don't go as you anticipated?
* Are you capable of attracting people smarter than you to work on your business? Are you in a geographic location that has enough smart, ambitious people to make the company sing?

Product risk
* Are you solving the right problems?
* Is your product easy enough to use that your customers 'get enough juice for the squeeze?'
* Is anyone willing to pay for your product?

- Have you thought through the challenges that will come with increased usage?

Competitive risk
- Who else is tackling the problem?
- Why aren't they successful?
- How are you different?
- How will competitors respond to your entrance?

Financial risk
- Are there larger investors interested enough in the space to fund follow-on rounds?
- How much will you need to raise to be a 10x company?
- Who else has been funded and how much have they taken in?

Sales risk
- Do you know how to get someone on the phone?
- Can you generate leads without using your network?
- Can you create a pipeline that's 6x larger than what you need to close?
- Do your customers already have a line item in the budget to buy your product?
- Are there enough customers in your space to create a real business?
- Do you understand who buys and why?
- How change-averse or risk-averse are your buyers?
- Do your prospects acknowledge the pain, or do they have to be educated?

Putting your pitch together requires more than knowing your business and how to address the standard ten slides. It requires putting yourself into the shoes of someone who is inclined to do nothing and find ways to show the upside while mitigating the downside.

RESPONDING TO INVESTOR QUESTIONS

Every early company has a soft underbelly. The ones who get funded acknowledge it and have a plan to firm it up.

Your underbelly is the host of questions to which you don't have a great answer. These are the questions you hope aren't asked. You know the ones. Yet, they almost always do get asked.

These are the questions that are holding you back from getting funding. Until you confront why they're so thorny and what challenges they present, you're wasting your time raising money.

We get conditioned into responses. When we provide an answer to one of our soft underbelly questions, we believe we had a good answer if we're not met with resistance. We're wrong.

Most likely, the question was answered in a way that proved you have no idea how to overcome it or worse, that we don't want to face it. And there is no reason to ask a follow-up question when the first hurdle tripped us up.

Our misinterpretation of the lack of follow-up hurts us the next time as well because we double down on the non-answer that "got us through" the last time.

You can't dodge bullets.

Consider These Actions:
- Get help. You know the questions you fear. Ask the same pointed questions to others to see what their answers sound like. Ask prospects, mentors, investors, and your team. The answer is out there, you just have to find it.
- Go first. If you're pitching without a great response to the question(s), include a slide with known challenges. Ask the investors to whom you're pitching for their thoughts. Showing the gap in your knowledge shows you don't know everything but want to find the answer.
- Record yourself. See how you squirm when asked the question, how you evade eye contact, or dodge. Work on those moments over and over and over again so you act like a normal human being instead.

MAKING FUNDRAISING LESS PAINFUL

Fundraising is not fun.

You will get rejected a lot. It won't always feel like it because the rejection will come in the form of, "I love what you're doing and you have a great team. Let's talk again in a couple of months" or "It was awesome meeting you. I love what you're solving. Keep me updated on your progress."

The hours you invest demand a return. To keep yourself going and to continue adding value, those hours you spend with investors should be *your* hours.

What non-monetary return can the investor to whom you're pitching provide to you?

Introductions. Investors are nothing if not well connected to people with a lot of money. Those people often run other businesses who could potentially be a customer, partner, or future acquirer. Ask for an introduction. Slip your foot between the jamb and the door as its closing. It's always harder to say no in person than it is over e-mail. While it requires they use some social capital, if you present well and show the benefit to whomever you want to meet, you can get it.

Note: The one introduction you never want, however, is an introduction to another investor. Don't ask for them. Why would another investor be willing to throw money into your venture if you were introduced to them by somebody who they know and (presumably) respect, who wasn't willing to invest in you themselves? The signal it sends is, "This isn't good enough for us, but it might be for you." That's a terrible way to maintain a relationship.

Get operational playbooks. If you've targeted the investor because of their prior investments, it's well worth asking about the path to traction others took. For example, if pricing is your issue, they'll have seen the results of others' experiments.

Learn on their dime. Investors love patterns. If you can learn how their successful companies operated, you can draw a parallel to your own operations. Doing so allows you to later demonstrate there's a playbook ready to follow.

Uncover upcoming risks. Ask what risks they see in front of you that you haven't addressed. You will be better prepared for your next meeting and it may trigger an idea you can bring back to the team that adds another few tenths of a point to your odds of finding success.

Consider These Actions:

- Compete. Give yourself and your co-founder a scorebook. Give a point for getting a non-investor introduction, three for an idea to solve an operational challenge, five for using their analyst to build a model for you. Whatever it is, make it fun. Getting rejected sucks, so you need to find something that gets you over that next false summit.

- Bet. What's the reason the investor will tell you as to why you're rejected? Wants to see more traction? Isn't sure the market is ready yet? Because you're not located in their city? The rationale is a known, finite set so find the dark humor in it. Winner gets a company-paid upgrade to cattle-car plus on the flight home.

DODGING THE INVESTOR WHIPSAW

Pitching investors often feels like a game of 'guess what number I'm thinking.' You give your presentation while trying to roll in the feedback you've heard recently.

And then you hear something counter to the prior feedback.

It leaves you feeling like you're trying to guess the business model/feature/hire that will get the investment.

But everyone will have a different opinion. If you're scrambling to give the answer you think they want to hear, you're missing out on giving them the benefit of seeing who you are and how you think.

Pitching VCs should be like an athlete watching game film where each pitch is a play. No single play can tell you how to improve your performance. It takes dozens before you can confidently make adjustments.

In one pitch, you'll hear that you're trying to be too much to too many. In the next, you'll hear your market isn't big enough. And you gave the same pitch!

Objections are often contradictory and can leave you flailing from one stated approach to another, yet both can be true.

Until you get to the point where you can pitch confidently, state your approach, and support the rationale, investment will be hard to come by.

If you don't believe in an approach, nobody else will either. State your path and be comfortable knowing others will disagree.

Consider These Actions:
- Put as much thought into going to market as you have the solution to the problem. Though investors preach product–market fit, that doesn't drive dollars. Come up with an approach you believe in and bang that drum.
- Find friendly fire. Everyone will have an opinion about everything. It shouldn't be hard to find a couple dozen friendly investors, fellow entrepreneurs or someone who's sold to the same audience to take pot shots at your approach. Somewhere amongst all those conversations will be overlap that is a sensible approach to the particular problem you're solving.

- Look at how similar companies sell. Who are they targeting? Why? How are they reaching them? Does it make sense for your product? If something is working for someone in a tangential business, then there's a known model that your prospects have already accepted, even if your solution is different.

NAVIGATING THE TERM SHEET

Negotiating the deal to invest in your company can be brutal. Everything is a stiff breeze in your face.

Odds are, there isn't a lot of competition for your deal, which means you don't have any leverage. You're also learning about something for the first time, while your investors have negotiated hundreds of previous term sheets. They have analysts modeling out what their investment looks like in the next round and the round following.

Conversely, you're an outlier if you've put more than a few day's thought into your pro forma.

The leverage points used against you will tell you a lot about how your potential investors view you and your relationship. Those terms will also foreshadow their future behavior.

Though investors may wear your fleece vest, they're not really on your team. Negotiating your deal is on you and the more you know going in, the less that can be used against you.

"Sure, you'll own a smaller piece, but the pie is much bigger." This works in your favor only in the upper decile of outcomes. That's the outcome where you execute without making many mistakes and sales flow steadily enough to lead you to grow at least 70% annually. In most cases, a smaller piece of pie without the fruit filling is just crumbs.

"We're all in the same boat." Not really. Investor terms will always have preference to your own. The argument that you're in the same boat doesn't hold water. You may both be in things that float. But you're in a dinghy with only a set of oars to get you to shore while they helicopter on and off their adjacent yacht.

The term sheet isn't designed for you. The marketing story of pies and boats are to meant soften the edges, not reflect reality. Unless you have leverage to dictate terms, you should know the tactics that get used against you. These tactics favor the investment fund's LPs, not the asset they're looking to purchase.

You may not get materially better terms, but you at least know the game played against you.

- **The waiting game.** Time is always on the investor's side. If they wait a couple more months, they'll have more information on your ability to compete and your cupboards will be slightly less stocked. Thus, you become more likely to accept more onerous terms. Only a fool invests now when they can get the same product for less later.

- **Lack of competition.** It's hard to get one investor interested, let alone getting two or more to compete. The threat of being boxed out by another investor is slim and they know it. They also know you'll come back to negotiate terms if you do find another willing to invest.

- **The future.** Investors play a longer game. Very few investments are returned based on the first round. In the portfolio, a clear home run may be made here, but most will be the doubles and triples that are just as much a factor of their ability to negotiate investment terms as it is in your execution.

- **Preferences.** The difference between '*and*' and '*or*' is huge. While 1x liquidation preferences are common, the difference between 1x preference *and* participation and 1x *or* participation is likely millions of dollars. The former gives them their money back before they split proceeds with you, the latter gives them the option to get their money back or to split the proceeds with you. 'Or' at least puts their boat nearer yours.

Consider These Actions:

- Spend the money for good lawyers and lean hard on mentors. You want people who have negotiated a term sheet before and know the tricks.

- Model ahead. Know what happens to your equity stake in the next round based on various valuations. Be skeptical. Just like investors, you need to think longer term, too. Give on valuation today in exchange for limiting those painful triggers that crush you in the next round if you're not flawless.

- Use judo psychology. Many investors hold the view that people are monetarily driven. Use it against them. The simplistic view of motivational factors can play in your favor. Negotiate using the thinking that you need enough upside and to keep yourself motivated and salary to stay focused. Show them what you've modeled and ask what drives future motivation as the return gets smaller.

BUILDING A USEFUL BOARD

A board may feel like a necessary evil.

There are very few people, if any, to whom you will feel comfortable baring all the company's warts. You may not be able to admit them to yourself, so the idea of telling the board becomes laughable.

It's not because of a lack of trust or a desire to deceive, but because investment is a long game. Just as your investors won't tell you when their LPs are screaming and there's no likelihood of follow-on funding, you will inevitably hold something in reserve as well. You want their investment again, and so life is presented as being a little shinier when presenting to your board each month.

Should it be this way? No. Is it healthy? No. Does it happen? Yes.

Ultimately, a board is as effective as its independent board members. They are the most objective and usually have the most industry knowledge.

Form your board early. Find those independent board members with deep industry experience today. There are three good reasons for doing so.

Most importantly, they can help you focus on the important things that will drive revenue. They know how the buyer thinks and can help you shortcut the process by sharing their own prior experiments. Further, the earlier you hold yourself accountable to someone, the more progress you'll make.

Second, if you've done a good job of identifying excellent people in your industry, then you'll most likely get to retain the seat you've already filled after investment has been secured. The incentives aren't necessarily misaligned, and this person isn't 'your' vote, but the one who sources the independent seat may be slightly more likely to earn the benefit of the doubt in a dispute.

Third, the independent seat can hold sway over your investors. Fellow entrepreneurs who prove they're the experts at the table can help you drive decisions toward what makes the most sense for the business. Your investors will look to them, even if they don't realize it.

That seat is also the only one who doesn't have a direct financial stake in the company. That allows you to be more transparent with them than you could be with your investors.

That transparency can allow the independent seat to raise issues by framing them differently in order to get more productive and constructive discussion going. Instead of a pointed spotlight on your vulnerabilities, they can broach it via, "when we were at this stage, we faced [xyz]…"

Consider These Actions:

- Punch above your weight. Use a board seat to get someone in the loop who may not give your company a second thought without the obligation. It need not be a long-term attachment. Seats can always be re-evaluated annually.

- Be honest about your blind spots. Admit that revenue is what drives investments and assemble a small group of advisors who can help you drive dollars. Form an advisory group. You will likely find one or two with whom you click. Ask them to be independent board members.

- Keep independents close. Finding someone in the industry as an independent seat can buy you access to all sorts of potential rewards: pricing structures, prospect lists, introductions, hires, etc. With bi-weekly updates, you can earn trust and gain access to information that may otherwise be out of reach.

MANAGING THE BOARD MEETING

Board meetings are a pain in the ass—no way around it. But they are the one time a month or a quarter that you have this group of people around the table at the same time. And since you're required to be there, you may as well get something out of it.

First of all, your board meetings should happen outside the board meeting. Your goal should be to make the actual meeting itself perfunctory—checking the legally required box.

Board meetings could be as short as,

"Did you hit revenue targets this quarter?"
"We did."
"Will you again next quarter?"
"Yes. Our pipe is 7x our closing target."
"Great, see you next month."

Making meetings perfunctory requires sharing the same information you would in the group meeting individually throughout the time between gatherings. When you share that information, you can collect feedback without concern of facing a reactionary dog pile of ideas. You also give the board member time to process your solution without requiring an immediate response in front of a peer group.

Nothing should be a surprise. Ever.

Board meetings are populated with big egos. Big egos hate surprises because it can make them look bad. Even when you're right, you'll lose. Surprises suck the value right out of the room.

Know that, ultimately, your investors care about one thing—revenue (two, if you include next quarter's revenue).

Managing your board means managing their relationship to your revenue. How you handle that depends on each of their personalities. Because they will all react differently, you want to highlight where revenue stands relative to goals in one-on-one sessions ahead of time.

One personality is easier to deal with than three-to-six, simultaneously.

If you're going to miss, absorb any frustration they have out of sight of the rest of the board members. Removing emotion from the boardroom will keep everyone focused on the business instead of themselves.

You'll be surprised how little is remembered in between meetings and how little they actually know about your business. They have a half dozen other companies they're trying to keep on the rails and hear dozens of pitches in between meetings with you. While some may keep it all straight, assume they don't and can't. That means repeating your plan, repeating where you are at within the plan, repeating what's next, repeating how you're evaluating success, and repeating when you'll know you need to do something differently.

You can't repeat it all enough.

Use one-on-one time to do that and to probe for new objections to your plan. Noting objections ahead of time will give you a chance to think them through and come back with a response instead of reacting off the cuff. Telling someone their idea won't work is far easier out of earshot of their peers.

Consider These Actions:
- Be consistent. Schedule regular one-on-ones with each board member between meetings. Don't cancel them. Have the same agenda. Repeat, repeat, repeat.
- Play to your investors' strengths. Use your scouting report on them to make an ask. Can they help keep another board member on the rails? Can they talk through personnel issues? You know where they're useful. Steer their actions toward their strengths.
- Nothing (or very little) you discuss in the board meeting should be new information to anyone. The board meeting should recap where you've been and reiterate what you're doing to drive revenue going forward. Structure your meeting so you know who holds which issue and pacify those as much as possible ahead of time.
- Restate each member's positions and objections with them privately ahead of time. You want them to remain consistent, so you aren't surprised in the meeting.
- Request help from each member ahead of the meeting. Everyone has their odd peccadilloes, not all of which are relevant to your company. When you know objections ahead of time, enlist others to help quell dissent (or to give you better ideas on how to solve them).

AVOIDING INVESTOR WEAKNESSES

It's up to you to know where each investor can contribute and how to use the others to close ranks on the one banging the table around something they know little about.

Every investor has their weaknesses; whether it's an inability to manage the rest of their own partners, inexperience with your industry, or a lack of operational experience. Your investors have weaknesses and biases that will hurt you. They won't do so intentionally, but unless you know what they are, you are far more apt to blindly follow poor 'advice' or allow disagreement to fester.

And when you have little revenue, you have little margin for error. You can't afford bad advice.

You alone can't manage this. Weaknesses have to be known by the rest of the board, so the group doesn't allow poor advice to rule the conversation simply because it was given more loudly.

Odds are, everyone subconsciously knows who knows what and will tune in or out based on the respect they have for the knowledge given. But you can't let them tune out. When others shut down or change the topic, the advice hangs in the air with an expectation that you will do something with it.

You need to have someone else to credibly acknowledge its existence and drive agreement that it is not an action item.

Planning your board meetings is more than knowing what you're going to say. It's minimizing pontification, personal grudges, haphazard ideas, and pet projects, all of which requires coordination.

Orchestrating that coordination effectively means knowing how to use the strengths of some to minimize the weaknesses of others.

Consider These Actions:
* Casually ask your investors for their strengths and weaknesses. They'll likely be blind to their weaknesses, but you can always highlight when something falls outside of their self-described strength. It's tricky but having ground rules where everyone's strength is acknowledged can allow you to defer to those whose strengths address the issue raised.

- Identify strengths and weaknesses on your own and share with a board member(s) you trust. Vet the assessment and craft a plan to mitigate vocal contributions from areas of weakness. It may be a good cop/bad cop routine or just a magician's misdirection, but unless you're absolutely killing it, you need someone else who can step in and play bad cop for you. That trusted board member can also call upon others to quell unproductive discussion.
- Plan your board meetings. What do you want everyone to take away at each step of the discussion? Who will object to what, and how do you respond? If you know certain objections will arise, you can preemptively call upon the 'expert' prior to the board meeting and ask them to say a few words on a presented slide to prevent others from jumping in first.

UNDERSTANDING INVESTOR MOTIVES

Investors will get paid.

Their return is only realized when someone buys your company. There is no interest in a cash-flow business. Yet, the only way you can be completely in control of your own destiny is to create a real business that generates profits.

Most acquiring companies are trying to acquire growth, profits be damned.

And therein lies the rub.

Where you see value in creating a real business, the investor's portfolio approach and the need to get liquid for their LPs, demands your attention on the top line because that's where the outsized multiple lies.

When founding RoundPegg, I found myself at odds with our investors about the kind of revenue we generated. I had just closed our second largest deal ever with Nike and was feeling pretty good about extending our runway another few months while adding a blue-chip name under our umbrella.

The deal wasn't a bull's-eye, more like the next ring out from there. It was a consulting project centered around the output of our software rather than a SaaS deal for the software only. It was one-time revenue to prove our effectiveness. We got paid to do a case study which we could leverage into SaaS wins at Nike and well beyond.

That didn't change the one-time nature of the revenue.

Intellectually, I knew it wasn't as valuable, but I also had a longer-term view of its value.

At the next board meeting, the deal was met with yawns at best and frustrated criticism at worst from the investors (the independents were excited).

One investor, in particular, couldn't wrap his head around why I'd wasted time pursuing such a distracting deal.

None of his other portfolio companies played in our space, so he failed to grasp the legal risk we had to overcome in every sale. Similarly, his more successful investments were companies that performed transactional sales. They didn't require an evangelical approach to prove a different way of thinking.

Where I saw this as a steppingstone to more and better revenue later, he saw a one-time injection that didn't attract larger, follow-on investors who could protect his investment. Nor could this win help him support a larger paper valuation in his annual LP meeting.

Our motivations weren't just misaligned, but our time horizons were as well. It turned out his firm was about to start raising another fund. That required a need to show paper gains from the existing fund in order to raise the next. Paper profits have little value, but they're far more attractive than paper flat lines.

That was the last consulting deal I closed. I knew what the investors were saying was intellectually true, so I let his argument guide me. In hindsight, my naiveté hurt us. My job was to keep the company going, valuation be damned. Revenue is oxygen but I let myself get talked into thinking there was good oxygen and bad.

My failure to recognize our investors' motivations led to bad decisions and a long, slow, painful fade into an unappealing sale.

Consider These Actions:
Your investor is dealing with considerations that will influence his or her 'advice' to you, but they won't tell you what they are. The more you can understand the root of their challenges, the better you can address them in a way that meets their firm's needs and yours. And sometimes you just need to manage with a protective mechanism/escape path in mind.

- Hoard cash. Cash gives you options. The biggest cash consideration is headcount. Hire far more slowly than expected. Unless you have a good idea of how to generate revenue with more headcount, don't let the investor's presumptive rule of thumb that new investment should last 18-months dictate your hiring plans.

- Know where your investors are in their fund cycle. You are always better served being one of the earlier investments. The fund's seven-year clock is always ticking, no matter when you take their money. The earlier you are in their fund, the longer you have to prove your business. While you can't dictate when they invest, the knowledge alone is information you can use to understand how the partner thinks.

- Accept that unsexy dollars buy the same amount of time as the sexy ones. The more time you give yourself, the less dependent upon your investors' money you become. It may not eliminate misalignments, but it can minimize the amount of your time they consume.

- If you stray from your path, know why. In my case, I should have better explained why this fit a 'new' sales approach rather than arguing on the merits of runway. I'd learned a lot about the sales cycle and what was needed to take the next big leap but hadn't shared it.

FINAL THOUGHTS

Whether your idea is still on a napkin or in use by hundreds of companies, congratulations. You've taken the first step (or several) down a path which nobody has traveled before. Others may have traversed similar paths, but the forks they've opted to take along the way are and will continue to be slightly different. The conditions you create and the conditions you face will be unique to your company.

Know that there are many paths that lead to success. And even more that won't.

You'll choose the wrong path on occasion.

But also know that your steps can be retraced at every dead end. Or you may be able to cut through some bramble in order to step back on to the prior path. You can recover from nearly any decision, but you can't recover the time.

And the path to success will take a lot of time.

So, keep choosing the path that buys you the extra few minutes of life. It's in those few minutes that you can scoop up another thousandth or hundredth of a percent toward your odds of finding success.

Finally, be a good teammate to yourself. Just as the path we all take is different so, too, is how we define success. Own yours. Don't let the success of others change that definition or amplify the soundtrack that highlights your perceived shortcomings. Whoever you compare yourself to started at a different trailhead. Comparing your journeys is not fair to you.

As for that soundtrack, it tries its best to be crippling. Just knowing it's there and the tricks it plays is enough to turn the volume down. But it will remain a constant.

You'll have brief highs when you can't hear it. Relish those moments. Because, ultimately, the DJ is just flipping the record over. The soundtrack will return.

I don't mean to sound like Eeyore, but until you recognize it for the nonsensical noise that it is, you may start to believe it. Don't. It's just a tiny sliver of you that is afraid of what the world looks like when you succeed. There are enough hard things to tackle when starting something from a blank page. Don't stop yourself before others have the chance to. Who knows, you may find that nobody bothered to interfere and that you can see the pot of gold (or TED Talk, or the point your company's name is a verb, or whatever is your measure of success) at the end of the path you're already on.

I wish you the best. Nobody starts a business to make the world worse, so we need more people like you.

Good luck.

ACKNOWLEDGEMENTS

The soundtrack in my head is pretty deafening and it'd be crippling if not for my lead investor and wife, Andrea. Or, if I weren't reminded every day what love is and how cool it is to learn something new. Seeing the world through Max's and Rylan's eyes have made me both more patient with life and less tolerant of accepting the nonsense we self-manufacture. It's incredible to watch their minds process new situations and hear their thought processes. Helping them overcome their doubts and practice the mental game of life has made me stronger.

I also need to thank my dad, who has unfailingly supported my decisions, even when he knew they were poor ones, and my mom who built my empathy muscle by always getting me to see things through others' point of view.

On the professional side, I've learned that everyone has something to teach you, even if it's what *not* to do or how *not* to behave. Rather than fill another book with thanks, my LinkedIn connections have all contributed to this book—knowingly and not. But several people, over the course of my life, have given me advice and opportunities that have helped create a soundtrack of their own.

Scott Gilbert was an unwitting mentor who taught me that someone can lead while putting others first. Brad Carse showed me that the calm, rational voice carries farthest.

Carla Shull, who willingly put herself in the professional crosshairs and bought a (really bad) PowerPoint presentation, made my entrepreneurial journey real. Jeff Sneed showed me what it means to be a true professional sales executive, instilling in me the best pieces of advice I've ever gotten- "Brent, if you've closed a deal, just shut the hell up!".

The Boulder software startup community, especially in the early days, is enormously supportive and it wouldn't be what it is without hundreds, but Seth Levine, Brad Feld, David Cohen, Nicole Glaros, and David Mandell all unknowingly gave me a hand up along the way.

Jeremy Dillingham and Scott Hendrickson got me through some dark days while I was busy failing at a job for the first time. Their friendship and thoughtfulness still get me through the light ones, too.

All the founders who have listened to me talk in circles, like a dog looking to relieve himself, only to finally hit upon the point I wanted to make—thank you.

Toby Krout, Erin Stadler, José Vietez, Jack Donenfeld and the rest of the Boomtown folks, thank you for entrusting me with cohort after cohort. This book wouldn't have been written without the opportunity to talk through hundreds of the forks in the road with the teams you've vetted.

Chase Fraser, who has gone from 'a guy I once pitched' to a good friend who kept pushing for more in the process—all to my benefit—thank you.

Finally, everyone who touched this book to make it less bad, thank you – Ellen Neuborne and Katie Genauer, in particular, did things I couldn't have hoped to have ever done myself.